kraft•tex Style

kraft•tex Combines the Best of Leather & Fabric • Sew 27 Projects

Compiled by Roxane Cerda

stashBOOKS.

an imprint of C&T Publishing

Text, Photography, and Artwork copyright © 2014 by C&T Publishing, Inc.

Publisher: Amy Marson

Creative Director: Gailen Runge

Art Director: Kristy Zacharias

Editors: Lynn Koolish and Joanna Burgarino

Technical Editors: Debbie Rodgers and Gailen Runge

Cover Designer: Kristy Zacharias

Book Designer: Katie McIntosh

Production Coordinator: Jenny Davis

Production Editor: Joanna Burgarino

Illustrator: Jenny Davis

Photo Assistant: Mary Peyton Peppo

Styled photography by Nissa Brehmer and instructional photography by Diane Pedersen, unless otherwise noted

Published by Stash Books, an imprint of C&T Publishing, Inc., P.O. Box 1456, Lafayette, CA 94549

Library of Congress Cataloging-in-Publication Data

Kraft-tex style : kraft-tex combines the best of leather & fabric - sew 27 projects / compiled by Roxane Cerda.

    pages cm

ISBN 978-1-60705-910-3 (soft cover)

1. Leatherwork. 2. Sewing. 3. Leather, Artificial. I. Cerda, Roxane.

TT290.K73 2014

745.53'1--dc23

                    2014005998

Printed in China

10 9 8 7 6 5 4 3 2 1

Contents

All about kraft·tex 4

Care and feeding • Machine and hand sewing • Hand embroidery •
Cutting and embossing • Creasing, scoring, and folding • Adding color and
texture • Making the projects in this book

All about
kraft•tex

kraft•tex is versatile, durable, and, most of all, fun to work with. It's an eco-friendly paper-based material that is a wonderful substitute for fabric, leather, or vinyl. And it is perfect for portions of projects, such as the bottoms of bags, corners, handles, straps, and the like, that will take a beating when used regularly. It also makes a great transition from fabric to hardware, as on Heather Givans's Vintage-Inspired Camera Strap (page 88).

Developed as a replacement for natural leather in appropriate applications, kraft•tex is greener than vinyl and clearly more animal friendly than leather. kraft•tex is 100% recyclable. The plant used to produce kraft•tex is registered in the DIN EN 16001 Energy Management System, which, among other things, is an aggressive program to manage natural resources, conserve energy, and reduce carbon dioxide emissions.

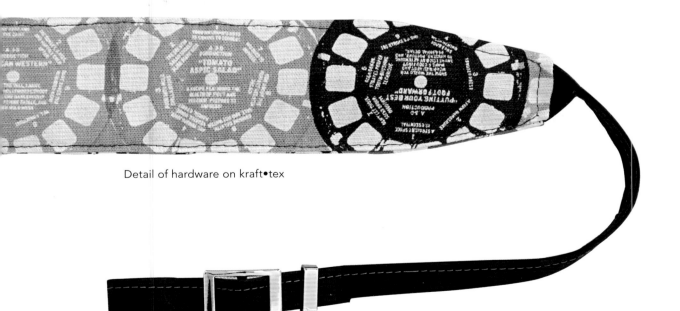

Detail of hardware on kraft•tex

Care and Feeding

kraft•tex can be machine washed and dried. If you are combining kraft•tex with fabric or trim and are planning to wash your finished piece, be sure to prewash and dry *all* pieces before cutting and sewing.

Directly out of the package, kraft•tex is smooth and a little stiff, which is ideal for projects in which you want a crisp, paperlike appearance, such as on the Super Fussy Frame Necklace (page 83) or the Snowflake Wallhanging (page 22).

Detail of die-cut kraft•tex snowflake

However, many of the designers whose projects are featured in this book said that they truly fell in love with the material after they washed it. It's colorfast, so you can toss it in with your regular loads of laundry and wash it a number of times for even more suppleness.

kraft•tex requires no special care, making it super easy to incorporate into any project without worry. It can be ironed on any setting without burning. And several designers found that kraft•tex wipes clean from most spills, making place mats and table runners no-brainer projects for this material. Jen Carlton Bailly even smeared a finished piece with blackberry jam, and it still wiped clean!

Machine and Hand Sewing

kraft•tex can be sewn by hand or by machine. When sewing two or more layers together, consider using a heavy-duty needle. Designate a sewing machine needle for use with kraft•tex and store it pinned to a scrap of kraft•tex when not in use.

Because kraft•tex perforates (similar to vinyl), it is best not to sew back and forth in one place too many times, or the material will tear. To secure the stitching at the beginning of a seam, place the presser foot and needle about ¼˝ in along the seamline, then stitch *backward* to the edge, and then proceed to sew forward along the seamline.

Machine stitching can look very decorative on kraft•tex. Check out Jen Carlton Bailly's Tech Stand (page 34) or Rachael Gander's Pocket Folders (page 26) for some great examples of how stitching can add detail and interest to your finished piece.

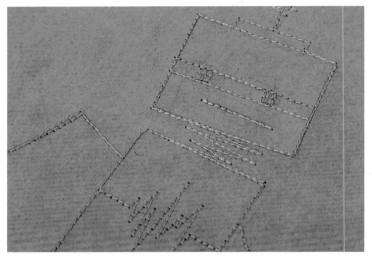

Detail of machine stitching

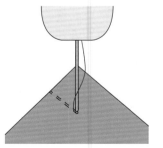

Start ¼˝ from beginning; stitch backward to edge and then forward.

Tip

Experiment with perforating! Try some of the decorative stitches on your sewing machine without thread for fun, quick, and easy embellishment.

When working with kraft•tex, don't use pins, as they will leave visible holes in your finished project and will also likely distort the shape and cause your pieces to come together unevenly. Instead of pins, you can use quilting clips, paper clips, binder clips, basting glue, or glue dots.

Hand Embroidery

You can hand embroider directly onto kraft•tex. Use the thinnest needle that will accommodate your desired number of strands so that the needle holes will not be overly visible. kraft•tex is stiff enough that you don't need to use an embroidery hoop. Check out Alyssa Thomas's Vegetable Basket Place Mats (page 10) and Zippered Pouch (page 61) or Rachael Gander's Pocket Folders (page 26).

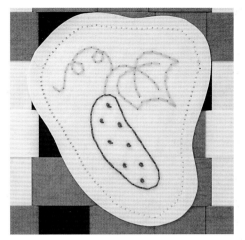

Detail of hand embroidery

Cutting and Embossing

You can cut kraft•tex with anything that cuts fabric or paper. You don't have to have specialized leather tools or knowledge to work with it, but you can still get the look of leather. You can create with it using basic tools that most crafters/sewists have at home—scissors, sewing machine, craft knife, die-cutting machine, embossing tools, punches, and more.

Creasing, Scoring, and Folding

Creasing, scoring, and folding can help you achieve the desired look or functionality in a finished project. Scoring before folding also ensures a more polished look to your finished piece. Folding without first scoring can result in wrinkling along the fold and uneven folds.

To score, simply place a ruler along the desired fold line and run your preferred scoring tool, such as a bone folder or dull butter knife, along the edge of the ruler, applying firm and steady pressure as you go. The kraft•tex will then fold easily along the line, without wrinkles or bumps.

Tip

kraft•tex is a paper product, and, like all paper products, it tends to dull blades. It's best to designate a pair of scissors or a rotary cutter to use only on paper products and another to use strictly for fabric.

Adding Color and Texture

Distressing

There are many ways to distress kraft•tex to add texture and a worn, weathered look—you can wash it, crumple it, burn the edges, and sand the surface with sandpaper.

Other Decorative Options

You can also try the following:

- Print on it with an inkjet printer.

- Paint it with acrylic paints.

- Dye it with COLORHUE or Procion MX dyes.

- Color it with shoe polish.

- Wax it with paste wax.

- Ink, draw, and stamp on it.

Making the Projects in This Book

- Unless otherwise stated, yardage for kraft•tex assumes a roll width of 18˝–19˝.

- If the designer has not indicated otherwise, the project can be either hand sewn or machine sewn on a standard machine.

- All projects assume you have a basic understanding of sewing and have handy a needle, thread, scissors, and basic sewing supplies.

That said, have fun! Be creative! Use the projects in the book as a starting point for your own creative adventures. kraft•tex will add a whole new range of options for your crafting and sewing projects.

At Home

Vegetable Basket Place Mats

Finished place mat: 18˝ × 13˝

Can you ever have too many place mats? Especially ones that are almost indestructible? Woven from strips of kraft•tex, with just a touch of embroidery, these place mats certainly fit the bill.

MATERIALS AND SUPPLIES

Makes 4 place mats.

- **kraft•tex:** 4 yards* total of one color or mix and match colors for weaving
- **kraft•tex (white):** ⅓ yard* for embroidery appliqués
- **Double-fold bias tape, ½˝ wide:** 7½ yards (purchased or make your own)
- **Embroidery floss** in orange, lime green, purple, ecru, red, emerald green, and white
- **Masking tape**
- **Scissors**
- **Carbon or graphite transfer paper**
- **Embroidery needle**

* Three packages of kraft•tex will be plenty for 4 place mats and the appliqués.

CUTTING

kraft•tex for weaving
- Cut 52 strips 1˝ × 20˝.
- Cut 64 strips 1˝ × 17˝.

Artist:

Alyssa Thomas

Alyssa Thomas is an illustrator, designer, author, and artist. Alyssa earned a Bachelor of Fine Arts degree in graphic design from the Minneapolis College of Art & Design in 2002. She has worked as a product designer for the children's apparel and stationery industries and illustrated the children's picture book *No Monster Here*. Alyssa started her company, Penguin & Fish, as a hobby to create lovely and quirky hand embroidery and sewing patterns and artful plush stuffed animals. Today, Penguin & Fish's products can be found in stores world-wide. Alyssa designs fabric for Clothworks Textiles and recently released her first craft book, *Sew & Stitch Embroidery*, about making hand embroidery the "star" of your next sewing project.

Company: *Penguin & Fish*
Websites: *penguinandfish.com, facebook.com/penguinandfish*

INSTRUCTIONS

Refer to All about kraft•tex (page 4) for basic information.

Weaving the Place Mat

1. Place the 13 strips 1″ × 20″ next to each other vertically on a flat surface, making a 13″ × 20″ rectangle. Tape down the top edges of the strips to hold them in place.

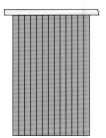

Tape top edges of strips.

2. Weave a 1″ × 17″ strip over and under the 13 vertical strips. The horizontal strip will stick out on both sides of the vertical strips. Push the woven strip up against the tape.

3. Continue weaving using 16 strips for each place mat. Push each woven strip up toward the top as you weave.

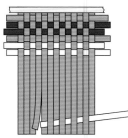

Weave place mat.

4. Tape over the strip ends along the 3 remaining edges. The tape will temporarily hold the place mat together. Carefully remove the taped place mat from your work surface.

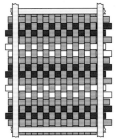

Tape remaining edges.

5. Sew around the place mat along the outermost strips, ⅛″ from the edge. Remove the tape. Trim along the outermost strips, cutting off all the ends.

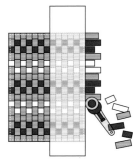

Sew around place mat, remove tape, and trim edges.

Adding the Bias Tape Edge

1. Open the end of the bias tape, fold over the end ¼″, and press. Refold and press again.

2. Open the bias tape and place the center fold of the tape along the edge of the place mat, starting at least 5″ away from a corner. *(Note: If you are using purchased bias tape, make sure the slightly narrower edge of the bias tape is on the top.)*

3. Sew the bias tape to the place mat, starting at least 2″ from the end of the bias tape, leaving a tail. Hold the bias tape along the edge as you sew or use paper clips to hold it in place. Sew to the edge of the mat and clip the threads. Do not backstitch.

Sew bias tape to first side, leaving 2″ tail at start.

4. Fold the bias tape around the corner of the place mat, keeping the center fold of the bias tape on the second side of the place mat edge. Tuck the folds, creating a mitered corner on both sides. Sew along the second side of the place mat, starting at the inner mitered corner.

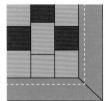

Start sewing at inner mitered corner.

5. Continue sewing the bias tape to the place mat. Stop sewing a few inches before you reach the starting tail of the bias tape. Cut the end of the bias tape so that it overlaps the tail by 1″. Place the cut end along the side edge of the place mat; then place the starting tail over it. Continue sewing over the ends to your starting point.

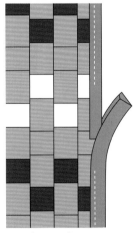

Overlap ends.

Stitch and Color Guide

Lines: backstitch
Dots: french knots

Lines: backstitch

Lines: backstitch
Leaves: single chain stitch

Thin lines: backstitch
Thick lines: chain stitch
The color blue represents white floss

Stitching the Embroidery

Note: Stitch as many embroidery designs per place mat as desired.

1. Using the carbon or graphite transfer paper, transfer the embroidery designs to the white kraft•tex. Make sure to leave at least 2″ of space between the designs.

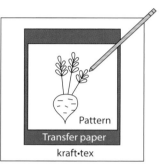

Transfer embroidery designs.

2. Embroider the designs, referring to the Stitch and Color Guide. Because of the stiffness of the kraft•tex, you don't need to use an embroidery hoop. You may, however, want to pre-poke the stitch holes as you go.

3. Cut around the embroideries, at least 1″ away from the stitches.

4. Position the embroideries on the place mat. Hold each embroidery in place with a couple of pieces of tape. Carefully sew the embroideries to the mat using a ¼″ seam allowance.

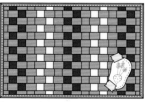

Sew embroidered appliqué on place mat.

Embroidery Designs

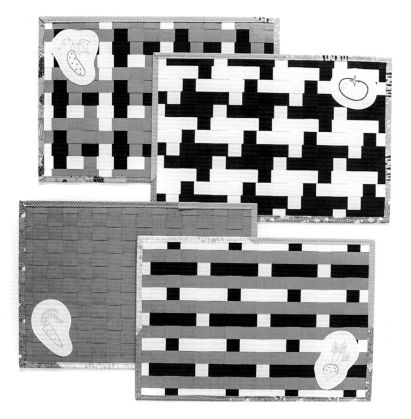

Sweet Storage Boxes

Finished boxes:
2˝ wide × 2˝ long × 2˝ tall
3˝ wide × 3˝ long × 3˝ tall
4˝ wide × 4˝ long × 4˝ tall
3˝ wide × 10˝ long × 2½˝ tall (flatware tray)

Being organized is important, but who says organization needs to be boring? These sturdy little kraft•tex boxes with fabric liners make sorting and storing fun. They are made for everyday use but can also pretty up special occasions. Change the liner to suit your decor or the festivity. Use your imagination—and your lifestyle—to decide how many boxes to make. You can customize the sizes too!

MATERIALS AND SUPPLIES

- **kraft•tex:** 1 roll (19″ × 1½ yards)
- **Fabric:** Use the cutting instructions to determine the amount required for your desired box size(s).
- **Paper-scoring tool** (I like Alex Anderson's 4-in-1 Essential Sewing Tool.)
- **Pencil**
- **Craft glue**
- **Paper clips**
- **Self-healing cutting mat and ruler**

Optional

- **Decorative-edged scissors**
- **Alphabet stamps**
- **Ink pad**

Artist:

Kristyne Czepuryk

Kristyne Czepuryk has always been a crafty girl. Over the years she has dabbled in everything from scrapbooking to macramé, decoupage to garment making, and almost every form of needlework (although she favors quilting and embroidery). Whenever she sees something interesting, she figures out how to make it. As long as she's making something, she's happy. She is the author of *S is for Stitch*, published by Stash Books.

Company: *Pretty by Hand*
Website: *prettybyhand.com*

CUTTING AND SCORING

Use the chart below to cut and score the materials for your desired box size.

	Finished box size	kraft•tex piece	Score line distance from edge	Fabric piece	Corner square cut size
Cube	2″ × 2″ × 2″	6″ × 6″	2″	9″ × 9″, including 1″ cuff	3¼″ × 3¼″
	3″ × 3″ × 3″	9″ × 9″	3″	15″ × 15″, including 2″ cuff	5¾″ × 5¾″
	4″ × 4″ × 4″	12″ × 12″	4″	18″ × 18″, including 2″ cuff	6¾″ × 6¾″
	5″ × 5″ × 5″	15″ × 15″	5″	21″ × 21″, including 2″ cuff	7¾″ × 7¾″
	6″ × 6″ × 6″	18″ × 18″	6″	24″ × 24″, including 2″ cuff	8¾″ × 8¾″
Flatware tray	3″ × 10″ × 2½″	8″ × 15″	2½″	14″ × 21″, including 2″ cuff	5¼″ × 5¼″

INSTRUCTIONS

Refer to All about kraft•tex (page 4) for basic information.

Making the Box

1. Cut out a piece of kraft•tex using the Cutting and Scoring chart or the instructions in Cutting the kraft•tex (page 19).

2. Score the fold lines using a ruler and a paper-scoring tool by lining up the ruler along an edge using the appropriate measurement from Cutting and Scoring or the instructions in Scoring the kraft•tex (page 19).

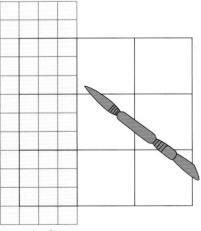

Score kraft•tex.

Calculating Custom Sizes

It's easy to make these boxes in custom sizes to fit your particular needs.

Cutting the kraft•tex

To cut a custom-sized box, decide on the finished width, length, and height of the box and use the following formula to determine the cut size dimensions:

Cut width = (width + (2 × height))˝

Cut length = (length + (2 × height))˝

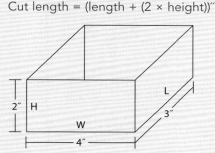

For example, to make a box that is 4˝ wide × 3˝ long × 2˝ high, cut a piece of kraft•tex 8˝ × 7˝.

4˝ (width) + (2 × 2˝ (height)) = 8˝

3˝ (length) + (2 × 2˝ (height)) = 7˝

Scoring the kraft•tex

To score a custom-sized box, score a line on each side that is the same distance from the outside edge as the desired height of the box.

Using our example, the box is 2˝ tall, so score a line 2˝ from each outside edge of the kraft•tex piece.

Cutting the Fabric Lining

To make a custom-sized fabric lining, decide the depth of the finished cuff and how much you need for the hem. Then use the following formula:

Fabric width = (kraft•tex width + (2 × cuff) + (2 × hem))˝

Fabric length = (kraft•tex width + (2 × cuff) + (2 × hem))˝

For example, using our sample kraft•tex measurement (8˝ × 7˝) for a lining with a 2˝ cuff and a 1˝ hem (½˝ turned under twice), we would cut the fabric 14˝ × 13˝.

8˝ (width) + (2 × 2˝ (cuff)) + (2 × 1˝ (hem)) = 14˝

7˝ (length) + (2 × 2˝ (cuff)) + (2 × 1˝ (hem)) = 13˝

The fabric lining pieces have squares cut out of all 4 corners. The formula for the square size is as follows:

((fabric width – box width) / 2) – ¼˝

Using the previously determined fabric and box sizes, cut a 4¾˝ square from each corner.

((14˝ (fabric width) – 4˝ (box width)) / 2) – ¼˝ = 4¾˝

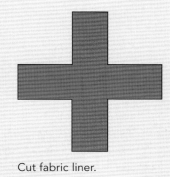

Cut fabric liner.

3. With a ruler and pencil, draw a diagonal line through each corner square and draw an X on the inside triangles to indicate the part that will be cut away.

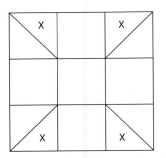

Draw lines through corners and mark cutouts.

4. Cut out the triangles along the pencil line and the scored line.

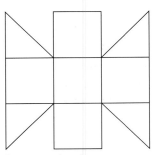

Remove triangles.

5. Fold each scored line toward the middle of the box. Reinforce each fold using a ruler and the scoring tool.

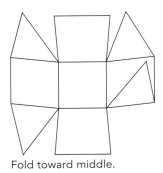

Fold toward middle.

6. To shape the box, apply a thin layer of glue to the corner triangles.

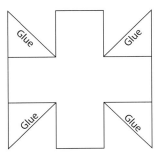

Apply glue to corner triangles.

7. Fold up the sides, making sure the diagonal cuts are visible from the outside of the box. Press the glued triangles to set them. Hold the sides together with paper clips until the glue is dry.

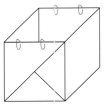

Glue and clip sides.

Making the Lining

1. Cut out a piece of fabric and cut away the 4 corner squares using the Cutting and Scoring chart (page 18) or the instructions in Cutting the Fabric Lining (page 19).

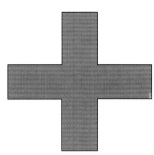

Cut fabric liner.

2. To form the liner, bring together both sides of the same corner, right sides together, and sew using a ¼″ seam. Repeat for the remaining 3 corners. Press the seams open.

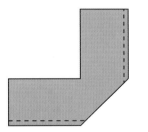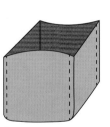

Sew corners.

3. Hem the top edge by turning and pressing a ½″ fold around the top, wrong sides together. Turn and press a second ½″ fold. Pin and sew the hem in place using a scant ½″ seam. For smaller boxes, use a narrower hem. The 2″ box here uses a ¼″ hem folded twice.

Hem liner.

4. Insert the liner into the box as shown. Fold the cuff over the outside of the box.

Insert liner into box.

Making a Label

1. Referring to the labels in the photos, use a pair of decorative-edged scissors to cut a rectangle of kraft•tex approximately 1″ × 2″. Using a pair of straight-edged scissors, cut a rectangle of kraft•tex approximately 1½″ × ¾″.

2. Glue the smaller rectangle to the center of the larger rectangle and apply words to the label using rubber stamp letters and ink.

3. Glue the label to either the side of the box or the fabric liner, making sure it is centered.

Snowflake Wallhanging

Finished wallhanging: 17″ × 17″

Finished coaster: 4″ × 4½″

with Bonus Coaster

This snowflake wallhanging goes together quickly and easily and is a fun way to add some hand-crafted holiday spirit to your seasonal decor. Experiment with different colors, stitches, and shapes. How about a Halloween-themed wall-hanging with black kraft•tex spiders on candy-corn-colored felt? Or a cute Easter wallhanging with white kraft•tex eggs (individually decorated, of course!) and pastel felt squares? Let the season be your guide.

MATERIALS AND SUPPLIES

- **kraft•tex (white):** 1⅛ yards or 1 roll

- **Felt squares, 5˝ × 5˝:** 9 in assorted blues, grays, and off-whites, plus 1 red for coaster

- **Die cutter and snowflake die** (I used a 4¼˝ diameter die from Sizzix.)

- **Corkboard:** 5½˝ × 5½˝ (*optional, for the coaster*)

- **Gluestick**

CUTTING

kraft•tex (white)

- Cut 1 square 17˝ × 17˝ for base.

- Cut 4 strips 1˝ × 19˝ for frame.

- Cut 1 strip 1˝ × 12˝ for hanging loops.

- Cut 1 square 5½˝ × 5½˝ for coaster.

- Die cut 9 or 10 snowflakes. (I used 9 total—8 for the final layout and 1 for the coaster. You may use 9 in the wallhanging if you prefer.)

Artist:
Betsy La Honta

Crafting, creating, and sewing since she started making paper dolls and Barbie clothes as a child, Betsy La Honta loves to figure out ways to get the project ideas in her head to translate into (hopefully!) beautiful, practical, and well-crafted items. After a ten-year journey running her own craft business (very handy while raising kids), Betsy is now happily employed with a great team at C&T Publishing and spends her days trying to focus on her actual job without getting *too* distracted by all the amazingly creative people, books, products, and ideas that are constantly bouncing around the office. (And yes, that *is* as hard as it sounds.)

INSTRUCTIONS

Refer to All about kraft•tex (page 4) for basic information.

1. Arrange the felt squares in a 3 × 3 grid, mixing the colors to get a pleasing arrangement.

2. Arrange the die-cut snowflakes on top of the felt squares in a random fashion, with some of the snowflakes hanging partially off the felt. Play around until you find a nice balance. Then sew each snowflake to its square, stitching from the center out to each section of the snowflake. Trim any part of the snowflake that extends over the edge of the felt.

Tip

Take a photo of your layout before you start sewing on the snowflakes. That way, if you get the squares mixed up or turned around, you'll have a photo to refer to.

3. Place the center felt square in the middle of the 17″ × 17″ kraft•tex base, measuring 6″ from all the edges of the base to make sure it is placed exactly in the center.

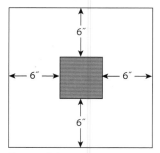

Center felt square.

4. Using a gluestick, tack the felt square to the kraft•tex so that it stays in place while you take it to the sewing machine. *Avoid putting any glue on the outer half of the square.* Repeat with the other 8 felt squares, working outward from the center square and butting the edges of the felt squares together so no kraft•tex shows beneath the felt. Starting at an edge, topstitch ⅛″ from the edges of the felt squares, all the way across the 3 squares. Repeat for all 4 rows across and 4 rows down, and then all around the edges of the outer 8 felt squares.

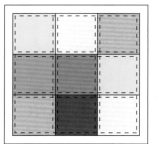

Topstitch felt squares.

5. Make the framing pieces by sewing a decorative stitch down the center of each of the 1″ × 19″ kraft•tex strips. I used a snowflake-like stitch available on my sewing machine. Trim each strip to ¾″ wide and 16¾″ long, centering the decorative element. (It is easier to sew it and then trim to size, rather than trying to center the decorative stitching exactly on a ¾″ strip of kraft•tex.) Trim each end to a 45° angle to create mitered corners.

Trim for mitered corners.

6. To make the hanging loops, sew down the center of the 1″ × 12″ strip with the same decorative stitch used on the frame. Then top-stitch ¼″ from each long edge. Trim the strip to ¾″ wide and cut the strip in half so you have 2 pieces ¾″ × 6″. Create a loop with each piece so you have 2 loops.

Topstitch hanging loops.

7. Center and clip a frame piece to a side of the base (not the top edge) ⅛″ from the felt. Topstitch along both edges of the framing strip. Repeat for the bottom and the other side framing strips, making sure the 45° angles butt together to create neat corners.

8. Clip the last frame piece to the top of the base. Place the hanging loops on the back side, with one positioned 2″ in from the left edge and the other 2″ in from the right edge, and the ends of the loops 1″ below the top edge. Clip in place. Topstitch the frame piece to the base as in Step 7, stitching the loops on at the same time.

Bonus Project: Coaster

INSTRUCTIONS

1. Sew a die-cut snowflake to the center of a 5″ × 5″ square of felt.

2. Trim the square to fit the snowflake.

3. Sew the felt piece to the 5½″ × 5½″ kraft•tex (white) square.

4. Trim the edge to ⅛″. Glue to the piece of cork and trim to ⅛″ larger than the kraft•tex.

Pocket Folders

Finished folder: 9½″ × 12″

Rabbit embroidery design by
Marisa Ann of Andover Fabrics
and Creative Thursday

Tired of those boring old paper folders? These folders are perfect for all your storing and organizing needs. Decorate the outside any way you like and make the inside pockets and flaps to fit your needs. With kraft•tex, these folders will last forever.

MATERIALS AND SUPPLIES

- **kraft•tex:** 1 yard
- **Rotary cutter**
- **Craft knife,** such as an X-ACTO
- **Quilter's ruler**
- **Hand sewing needle and embroidery floss** (optional)
- **Lesley Riley's TAP Transfer Artist Paper** (optional, see Resources, page 119)

CUTTING

kraft•tex
- Cut 1 piece 18˝ × 30½˝.

Artist:
Rachael Gander

Rachael Gander is a sewist, mom, wife, designer, blogger, and fabric enthusiast who learned to sew alongside her mom but lost interest until her early twenties. She has spent the last fifteen years making up for lost time, experimenting with modern quilting, garment sewing, pattern design, hand-printed fabric, and textile design. Along with documenting her creative journey on her blog, imagine gnats, Rachael sells her original sewing and embroidery patterns in the imagine gnats shop.

Company: *imagine gnats*
Website:
imaginegnats.blogspot.com

Tip

Use an X-ACTO knife in the corners for accuracy.

Note

If you plan to hand embroider or use machine-stitch sketching on the folder cover, complete your stitching prior to continuing with the folder assembly (see Embellishments, page 29). TAP transfer can be done either before or after the folder is assembled (see TAP Transfer, page 29).

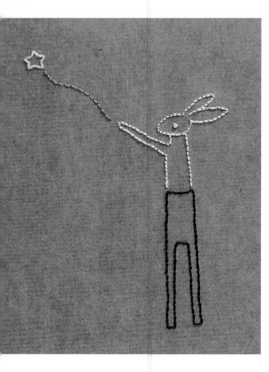

INSTRUCTIONS

Refer to All about kraft•tex (page 4) for basic information.

Folder Assembly

1. Draw measurement lines lightly with a pencil, following the pattern below.

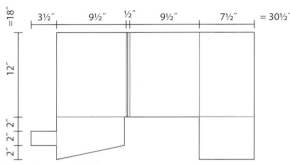

Draw lines on kraft•tex.

2. Cut around the outside of the measured lines with a rotary cutter. *Do not cut directly on the lines.*

3. Score the lines with a craft knife. To score properly, use the knife with a cutting motion but apply light pressure so that only the top layer of the material is cut. The lines will be scored on the outside of the fold line. Score the red lines as drawn. Score the blue lines on the reverse side.

4. Fold the 2″ × 3½″ tab and the 6″ × 7″ pocket to the outside.

5. Stitch the folded portions along the red lines.

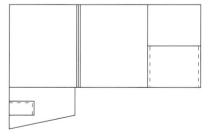

First pockets stitched

6. Fold the diagonal pocket up and the 7½″ × 12″ pocket to the inside. Stitch along the red lines.

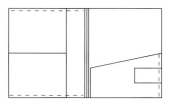

Stitch as indicated by red dotted lines.

7. Fold inside out at the center of the folder. Stitch on the interior, ¼″ from the folded edge.

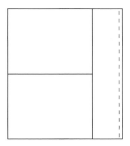

Stitch ¼″ from center fold as shown by red line.

8. Close the folder along this seamline and carefully erase any visible pencil marks.

Enjoy your folder!

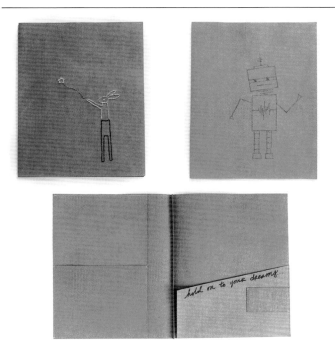

Embellishments

TAP Transfer

Follow the manufacturer's instructions to transfer your desired image onto the folder cover.

Transfer ideas

Use a favorite quote or a digital coloring page.

Hand Embroidery

1. Print the embroidery pattern in the desired size.

2. Place the printout on the cover of the folder, using painter's tape to hold it in place.

3. With a straight pin, "trace" the embroidery pattern by poking holes along the pattern lines, through both the pattern and the folder. Make the holes about ⅛″ apart.

4. Remove the embroidery pattern.

5. With a small, sharp hand needle and embroidery floss, backstitch through the poked holes to fill in the pattern.

Machine-Stitch Sketching

1. Lightly trace or draw your pattern onto the front cover with a pencil.

2. With a sewing machine, topstitch over all the pattern's lines.

Tip

Stitch over the lines multiple times in order to minimize starting new threads and to stitch as much of design as possible at once.

Penobscot Bay Travel Journal

Finished journal: 6″ × 9″

This painting technique reminds me of a sea chart of the islands in the coastal bays of the New England coast, which is why I named the project after Penobscot Bay. The journal has a replaceable writing pad and watercolor or sketching paper. Whether you are traveling on the high seas or exploring the high desert, record your trip in style with this beautiful travel journal.

MATERIALS AND SUPPLIES

- **kraft•tex (natural):** 9˝ × 14˝
- **Metallic acrylic paint:** 1 bottle each of light green and light blue (I used Lumiere paint.)
- **Medium-sized paintbrush**
- **Mid-weight clear vinyl:** 6˝ × 6˝
- **Black fine-tip Sharpie pen**
- **1⅛˝ button**
- **Blue or green beading cording or waxed linen:** 40˝
- **Assorted beads, including letters,** to embellish the cording (The beads must have a large enough hole for the cording to go through.)
- **Writing pad,** 5˝ × 7˝
- **Lightweight watercolor, sketchbook, or cardstock paper,** 8½˝ × 11˝: 5 or 6 pieces
- **Awl** or other sharp piercing tool
- **Craft knife,** such as an X-ACTO

Tip

You can purchase mid-weight clear vinyl in a craft store or salvage some from the packaging of things you've bought. The vinyl could also be omitted and another piece of painted kraft•tex could be used instead.

Artist:
Normajean Brevik

Normajean Brevik lives in a little seaside town on the coast of Connecticut. She and her husband, Odd, raised three children and own a local business. Her work is greatly influenced by the sea and her Norwegian heritage. She has written for many fiber and mixed-media magazines and books and believes that people grow as artists when they share their gifts. Nowhere is this more obvious than in the 1,000-person Internet group Fiber Art Traders that she started in 2005. She is available for teaching engagements around the globe.

Website: *groups.yahoo.com/ group/FiberArtTraders*
Email: *seasew@yahoo.com*

INSTRUCTIONS

Refer to All about kraft•tex (page 4) for basic information.

Scoring the Folds

1. With the kraft•tex in a landscape position, score a vertical line 2″ from the left.

2. Score a second vertical line 6″ from the left.

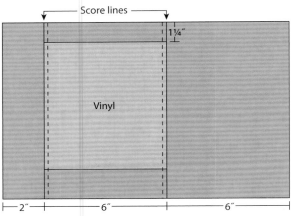

Score lines and vinyl placement

Painting the Journal

1. Apply the blue paint in a random pattern on the unscored side of the kraft•tex wherever you want "water."

2. Paint the remaining areas with green paint to represent the landmasses. Make sure the kraft•tex does not show through in any areas before you continue. Allow the paint to dry thoroughly.

3. Paint the inside cover in green and blue, to match the front, or in a solid color. Allow the inside cover to dry thoroughly.

4. With a fine-tip Sharpie pen, outline the green areas to define the landmasses. Add tiny islands and inlets. I try to shake my hand a bit as I draw the lines to give the coastline the jagged look of a sea chart. Make small and large islands, some hugging the coast and others farther out.

Journal Cover Assembly

1. Position the journal in a landscape position with the inside facing up and the 2″ score on your left. Place the 6″ × 6″ piece of clear vinyl 1¼″ below the top so that it lies between the 2 scored lines. Starting at the top, stitch to the bottom just inside the scored lines, making sure to stitch ⅛″ from the edge of the vinyl. Do this along both scored lines.

2. Fold the 5 or 6 watercolor, sketchbook, or cardstock papers 8½″ × 11″ in half as a unit so the pages are 8½″ × 5½.″ Use a bone folder or the handle of a kitchen knife to crease the fold; then trim the edges even with a craft knife. Using a sharp awl, pierce holes in the crease through all the layers 2½″ from both the top and bottom of the paper.

3. Place the fold of the pierced papers on the 6″ scored line, centering them between the top and bottom. Using the paper holes as a guide, pierce the cover. Thread the cording from the outside pierced cover through the papers on the inside. Pass the cording through the second set of pierced holes, to the outside of the journal. Tie the cords in a square knot so they won't slip.

4. Embellish the cords with beads and knot the ends.

5. Stitch the button on the outside small flap. Knot the thread several times as you stitch the button on.

6. Slip the cardboard back of the notebook through the vinyl to secure it in place. There will be room for you to hang a pen with a clip on the vinyl too.

7. Wrap the cording around the button to secure the journal once you have closed it.

Start recording your travels.

Tech Stand

Finished stand: 6½″ × 10½″

This easy-to-make stand will keep your tablet upright and easy to see. It's especially handy if you use it in the kitchen for recipes or for reading or even playing games.

MATERIALS AND SUPPLIES

- **kraft•tex:** 2 pieces 7″ × 11″
- **Muslin:** 5″ × 7″
- **80/12 Sharp needle**
- **Zipper foot**
- **Hand sewing needle**
- **Rotary cutter, cutting mat, and ruler**
- **Bag of rice, 16 ounces**
- **Fabric glue** (*optional*)

Artist:

Jen Carlton Bailly is a self-taught sewist who loves textiles, fashion, and art. She has a degree in fashion marketing from the Art Institute of Seattle, but sewing and quilting quickly became her addictions. Jen finds inspiration in everything from old dresser drawers to run-down Portland buildings. Currently working as the communications manager for the Modern Quilt Guild, she spends whatever free time she can squeeze in sewing. You can read about her crafty endeavors on her website.

Website: *bettycrockerass.com*

INSTRUCTIONS

Refer to All about kraft•tex (page 4) for basic information.

1. Stitch your design on the 2 pieces of kraft•tex. For mine, I stitched random straight lines in 2 colors.

2. With right sides together, sew with a ¼˝ seam allowance along a long and a short side. On the other long side, sew 3˝ of the seam, leave a 5˝ opening; then sew the remaining 3˝ of the seam.

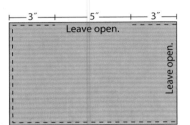

Stitch right sides together.

3. On the open short side, match the side seams to the center and sew with a ¼˝ seam.

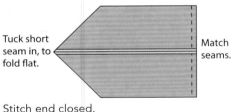

Stitch end closed.

4. Turn the piece right side out. If you have difficulty with this step, you may want to wet the kraft•tex to make it more pliable.

5. Fold the muslin piece in half crosswise to 2½˝ × 7˝ and sew all the sides together, leaving a small hole. Fill the bag with rice and then hand stitch the hole closed.

6. Insert the muslin rice bag and push it to the short, flat end. Sew across the kraft•tex to keep the muslin bag at the bottom and then sew 2 more rows ¼˝ apart.

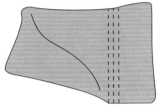

Sew muslin rice bag into one end.

7. Use a funnel to fill up the main part of the stand. You want it full. Hand stitch the opening closed or use fabric glue to close the seam.

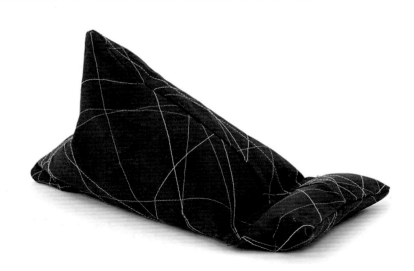

Bags

Saddle Bag Purse

Finished purse: 11¾˝ wide × 9¾˝ tall × 3¾˝ deep

Here's a purse you can take anywhere. There's loads of room for everything you need to keep close at hand. With kraft•tex, you can decorate it any way you like (I've included information on how I painted the kraft•tex), or you can let the natural beauty of the kraft•tex shine through. "Saddle up" and head out!

MATERIALS AND SUPPLIES

- **kraft•tex:** 2 yards (2 packages or 2 yards off the bolt)
- **Vinyl or pleather:** ¼ yard
- **Polyester batting:** ½ yard (I used Bosal Sew-In Fleece Style #326.)
- **Cotton fabric, such as quilting cotton:** ½ yard for lining
- **Contrasting cotton fabric:** ⅓ yard for pocket
- **Muslin:** ½ yard for interlining
- **Buckle:** 1½˝ wide for strap

Additional tools

- **Sewing clips** for holding kraft•tex and pleather
- **Rotary cutter, mat, and acrylic ruler**
- **Erasable pen**
- **⅛˝ hole punch** (I used a Clover punch.)

Painting and stamping (*optional*)

The following are the tools I used to paint and embellish the bag:

- **Gesso**
- **Sponge brush, 1˝:** 2 (1 for background and 1 for varnish)
- **Acrylic paints** (I used samples of acrylic interior wall paint from various paint companies.)
- **Paintbrushes with tapered tips** for fine designs
- **Stamping ink and stamps**
- **Gloss acrylic varnish**

Artist:
Cheryl Kuczek

Cheryl Kuczek is a designer of handbags, clothing, and home accessories. Her custom designs combine charm with a modern eclectic-vintage twist, using a mix of fabrics and trims. She launched her custom design business, Paradiso Designs by Cheryl Kuczek, in fall 2006. Since then she has published many patterns, including edgy clothing that works for all sizes and designer-like handbags, plus kits to make pleather handbag straps. She has also been published in many sewing magazines. Six years ago Cheryl began teaching adults and children not only how to sew but also how to incorporate their own styles into custom creations. Cheryl guides all of her students to complete their own projects and—even more important—to really understand design and the evolving creative process. She finds tremendous joy in the ability to inspire others with a reason to sew and create.

Company: *Paradiso Designs*
Website: *paradisodesigns.com*

INSTRUCTIONS

Refer to All about kraft•tex (page 4) for basic information.

Making the Patterns

Draw the rectangles specified below on paper or stiff plastic and cut out. Seam allowances are included.

1. For the Front/Back piece, draw a rectangle 12¾″ × 10¼″. On the top 12¾″ edge, measure in ⅞″ from each corner and mark a dot. Draw a line from each dot down to the lower corner below it. Erase the triangles on each side. This is the shape you will cut the Front/Back pieces.

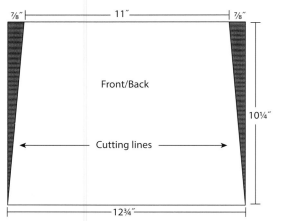

Front/Back pattern—Erase red triangles.

2. For the Flap, draw a rectangle 10¾″ × 10⅛″. On the top 10¾″ edge, measure in ⅞″ from each corner and mark a dot. Draw a line from each dot down to the lower corner below it. Erase the triangles on each side. This is the shape you will cut the Flap. Do not draw the inner rectangle yet.

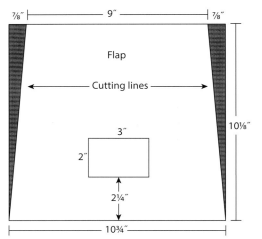

Flap pattern—Erase red triangles.

3. For the Side piece, draw a rectangle 4¾″ × 10¼″.

4. For the Bottom piece, draw a rectangle 4¾″ × 12¾″.

5. For the Flap Tab, draw a rectangle 3¼″ × 11⅝″.

6. For the Tab Holder, draw a rectangle 2″ × 4″.

7. For the Pocket, draw a rectangle 6½″ × 12¾″.

Painting and Preparing the Pieces

Painting the Background (*Optional*)

1. If you choose to prep with gesso, coat the entire surface of the kraft•tex with the gesso, using a sponge brush. Create texture with the strokes made by the sponge brush. For my bag, I used a crosshatch stroke.

2. Choose the background color and paint the background. I wanted mine to look like brown leather, but I added light pink and golden yellow for variety. I dripped some of each paint in different areas as I was painting the background, blending the yellow and pink into the brown as I continued to coat the background. Let the background dry thoroughly.

Painting the Pieces

1. Make a paper or plastic pattern for each pattern piece.

2. Trace around each pattern piece onto the painted kraft•tex. You will need the following pieces: 2 Flaps, 2 Front/Backs, 2 Sides, 1 Bottom, 2 Flap Tabs, and 2 Tab Holders.

For the Flap, do not draw the inner box that needs to be cut out yet—this will be done after the painting is finished.

3. Paint your design onto each pattern piece. Let the paint dry.

4. After the painting and embellishing are finished, position the Flap inner box. Draw a 3″ × 2″ box, centered on the Flap and 2¼″ from the lower edge. See the Flap pattern illustration (page 40). Do not cut the box out yet.

5. Coat the kraft•tex with varnish and let it dry for a day.

Tips for Stamping and Painting

- Stamping can be done on the raw kraft•tex. I would recommend varnishing any completed stamping designs to give them a protective coating. The raw kraft•tex will absorb the varnish, giving your stamped design a gloss finish.

- Some artists like to use gesso prior to painting, but you can also paint on the raw kraft•tex.

Cutting the kraft•tex Pieces

Use a rotary cutter and clear ruler to cut the kraft•tex and the pleather. This creates a neater edge than using scissors.

1. Using the patterns you created in Making the Patterns, cut 2 Front/Backs, Sides, Flaps, Flap Tabs, and Tab Holders, and 1 Bottom.

2. To add more texture, you can wash the pieces in a cold wash. Let the pieces dry in the dryer on a cool setting for 5 minutes. Lay them out to finish drying completely. If any paint or varnish rubs off, touch it up after the bag is completely constructed.

Cutting the Fabric and Batting

1. Cut 2 Front/Back pieces, 2 Sides, and 1 Bottom out of the lining, muslin, and batting.

2. Cut 1 Pocket piece out of the lining fabric and another out of the contrast fabric.

3. Cut a 2″ × 13″ strip from the contrast fabric for the Pocket trim.

4. Straighten a long edge of the pleather; then cut a 4½″ × 35″ strip for the Strap.

5. Trim ¼″ from the top edge of the batting Front/Back and Side pieces.

Preparing the Pieces

1. Layer the kraft•tex Side, Front/Back, and Bottom pieces with the matching batting pieces, making sure the batting is ¼″ from the top. Use a clip on each side to hold the kraft•tex and batting together.

2. Layer each set of the kraft•tex bag Flap, Flap Tab, and Tab Holder together and clip each side. *Make sure the sets cannot shift at all.*

3. Layer the Front/Back, Side, and Bottom lining pieces on top of the muslin interlining pieces. Pin with 2 pins on each side and on the bottom and 1 pin on the top, so that you'll know at a glance which side is the top.

Assembling the Bag

Seam *allowances are ½″ unless otherwise noted.*

The Strap

1. On the 4½″-wide pleather Strap, measure and mark 1½″ from the edge on the wrong side with an ink pen or a chalk roller.

2. Fold the opposite edge to this 1½″ line. Clip the folded edge in place.

3. Stitch ⅛″ from the fold; then fold the opposite edge to the line of stitching. Sew ¼″ away from the first line of stitching. Sew a third line of stitching ⅛″ away from the second stitching line.

4. Repeat the 3 lines of stitching from Step 3 on the other side of the Strap. Always start sewing from the same edge.

5. Cut the Strap piece into 2 lengths: 8″ and 27″.

6. On the 8″ Strap, use a hole punch or awl to make a hole in the Strap's center, 2″ from an end. Insert the buckle, putting the buckle center metal piece through the hole. Fold the 2″ end to the back of the buckle (make sure that the Strap fold is on the back). Sew ¼″ from the Strap end, through both layers of the Strap, to secure the buckle.

7. On the 27″ Strap, punch a hole in the Strap's center, 2¼″ from an end. Punch 4 more holes 1¼″ apart. On the end closest to the holes, finish the end by sewing across ⅛″ from the edge and again ¼″ away. Start stitching in the middle of the Strap, sew to the edge, reverse back across to the opposite edge, then sew back to the middle. Leave the other ends of both Straps straight and clean, ready to attach to the bag after the lining is sewn.

The Flap and Tab Holder

1. Starting in the top center of the Flap, sew both layers together ¼″ from the edges; then trim the edges ⅛″ from the stitching. Repeat for the Flap Tab (starting at the top center) and the Tab Holder (starting in the middle of a short side).

2. Using a rotary cutter and ruler, cut the Flap's center box edges, gently working up to the corners. Use scissors to finish cutting the corners. Sew around the box edges with an ⅛″ seam allowance.

3. Find the center of the top edges of the Flap and Flap Tab. Center the Tab on the Flap, clip the pieces, and sew them together using a ⅛″ seam allowance.

The Bag Exterior

1. On the Front of the bag, draw a 3¾″ × 1¾″ box, centered, and 2½″ from the top edge. Tape the Tab Holder on this box. Sew the short sides right on top of the original ⅛″ seam allowance. Start to sew in the middle of the sides and stitch to just over the edge, then back to the other edge, and then back to the center.

Tab Holder placement

2. On the wrong side of the 2 Front/Back and 2 Side pieces, mark a dot on the batting at the bottom corners, ½″ from the bottom and the side edges.

Mark dot at seam start points.

3. Clip the Front to a Side piece with right sides together. Starting at the bottom, 1″ from the edge, backstitch to the mark made in Step 2; then sew to the top of the bag and backstitch.

4. Trim the top edges so that they are even and trim the seam allowance at the top of the seam at an angle so it will not be seen at the top edge. This edge will be left as is and not turned under.

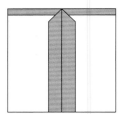

Trim seam allowance.

5. Flip to the right side and topstitch ⅛″ from the seam, starting at the bottom of the seam. Turn ⅛″ from the top to topstitch across the seam, and turn again to continue back to the bottom on the other side of the seam.

6. Repeat Steps 3–5 to attach the Back and remaining Side. The last seam you topstitch will be the most difficult, so take your time. Leave the bag with the right sides in.

7. Add the Bottom, right side up, to the right side of the bag. Match the side seams to the corners. With the seams open at the corner, the bag will form a square on the wrong side where the lining sides meet the Bottom at each corner. Clip into place.

8. Sew the bag Sides to the Bottom, making sure to turn each side's corner and catch the bottom of each side seam so there will be no opening left at the bottom of the corner seam.

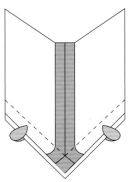

Stitch bag to Bottom piece.

The Lining

1. Pin the wrong sides of the 2 Pocket fabrics together.

2. On the wrong side of the Pocket, pin the 2″ × 13″ trim strip right side down (the strip will be longer than the Pocket top). Sew the strip to the Pocket with a ⅜″ seam allowance and press the trim and the seam away from the Pocket.

3. Fold down the unsewn edge of the trim to the raw edge of the seam and press the fold. Fold the pressed edge down again along the edge of the seam to the right side of the Pocket. Topstitch the trim to the front of the Pocket, ⅛″ from the folded edge.

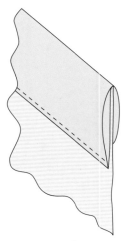

Fold trim to front and sew.

4. Find the center of the Pocket by folding it in half. Use a pin to mark the center at the top and bottom of the Pocket.

5. Pin the Pocket to the Back lining piece, matching the lower edges. Stitch the center seam from the bottom of the Pocket up to the trim. Once the trim has been reached, use a satin stitch to finish securing the Pocket to the Front/ Back. Repeat this stitching in reverse to stitch back to where you started. Trim the Pocket even with the sides of the Back piece.

Stitch centerline of pocket.

6. On the wrong side of the 2 Front/Back lining and Side pieces, mark the muslin at the bottom corners, ½˝ from the bottom and the side edges.

7. Pin the Front to a Side piece with right sides together. Starting at the bottom, 1˝ from the edge, backstitch to the mark made in Step 6; then sew to the top of the bag and backstitch.

8. Flip to the right side and topstitch ⅛˝ from the seam, starting at the bottom of the seam. Turn ⅛˝ from the top to topstitch across the seam, and turn again to continue back to the bottom on the other side of the seam.

9. Repeat Steps 7–8 to attach the Back and remaining Side, and add the Bottom like you did for The Bag Exterior (page 43).

10. Stitch ¼˝ from the edge around the top of the bag lining. Fold along this stitched line and press. Leave the lining wrong side out.

The Bag

1. Insert the lining into the kraft•tex bag, making sure that the Pocket of the lining is against the Back of the bag and the folded edge of the lining meets the edge of the kraft•tex. Match the corner seams and clip together at the top.

2. Sew around the top ⅛″ from the edge and again ¼″ from the edge.

3. Center the long Strap on the right Side of the bag, placing it 1¼″ below the top edge and making sure that the raw edge is toward the bag and not facing out. Tape the Strap in place and stitch ⅛″ from the lower edge, starting and ending in the middle of the Strap. Stitch again ¼″ from the edge, and finally for a third time matching the ¼″ topstitch at the top of the bag. Stitch the short Strap to the left Side of the bag in the same manner.

4. Find the center top of the bag Back and the top of the Flap. Mark a straight line in erasable ink at the bag Back and Flap top centers to match up for placement.

5. Line up the Flap topstitching line with the ¼″ top-stitching line on the bag Back, matching the center marks. Use painter's tape to hold the Flap placement for sewing. Stitch the Flap to the bag Back along the Flap topstitching line. Remove the tape gently.

Bag | Flap

Stitch flap to bag.

Yay—finished!

Indestructible Yoga Mat Sling

Finished sling: 16½˝ × 11½˝

Artist:
Carrie Bloomston

Carrie Bloomston is a mama, seeker, designer, abstract painter, and writer. After studying painting at the Rhode Island School of Design, she owned a decorative-arts/mural-painting company for sixteen years. Now, when not hanging out with her inspiring kids and thoughtful husband, she is working on her newest brand, SUCH Designs. Her family is her reason and her refuge. Carrie says expressing herself through art allows her to share joy and awe. She hopes to be an inner-artist enabler for others by sharing her designs.

Company: *SUCH Designs*
Website: *such-designs.com*

MATERIALS AND SUPPLIES

- **kraft•tex:** 1 yard
- **Nylon or cotton webbing:** 98″
- **Lighter or matches** to seal the ends of the nylon webbing
- **Carabiner** (*optional*)
- ⅛″ **nylon cording:** 13″ (*optional*)

CUTTING

kraft•tex

- Cut 1 rectangle 16½″ × 23¾″ for bag.
- Cut 1 rectangle 7½″ × 8½″ for pocket.

INSTRUCTIONS

Refer to All about kraft•tex (page 4) for basic information.

1. Turn the short ends of the 16½″ × 23¾″ rectangle under ⅜″. Press. Edgestitch ¼″ from the edge. Because kraft•tex is tough, you don't need to do this to the long edges.

2. Place the rectangle on a table right side up. Using a clear grid ruler, draw a faint pencil line 3½″ from each long edge to use as a guide when placing the straps. Set aside.

3. On the 7½″ × 8½″ rectangle, turn the top 8½″ edge under ⅜″. Press. Edgestitch ¼″ from the edge.

4. Center the pocket between the 2 pencil lines on the outside of the large kraft•tex rectangle, 1½″ from the top edge. Sew the bottom of the pocket in place, backstitching at the beginning and end of your stitching. The straps will secure the sides of the pocket. *Figure 1*

5. Using the pencil lines as a guide, place a cut end of the webbing in the middle of the large rectangle. Hold the webbing at this center and, following the line, bring it to the edge of the rectangle. Clip the webbing to the edge of the rectangle, then measure 24¼″ of webbing for the shoulder strap, and then clip it to the other side of the rectangle, just inside the pencil line. *Figure 2*

6. Keeping the webbing aligned to the *inside* edge of the pencil line, pin the webbing in place. *Don't overpin—you can use the pencil line to straighten as you work.* Continue up the other side, measure 24¼″ of webbing for the second shoulder strap, clip it to the bag, and bring the webbing back down to the starting point.

7. Beginning at the top of the bag, backstitch and sew along the inside edge of the webbing. Make sure you capture the pocket with the stitching. Turn around at the other end and come back up, backstitching at the end.

8. The webbing will overlap in the middle of the bag. If you are using nylon webbing, cut it so that it overlaps 1″ and use a lighter to sear the web so it won't fray. Repeat for the other side of the strap.

9. *Optional:* Loop the nylon cord around one handle and tie an overhand knot. Add a carabiner for holding your keys!

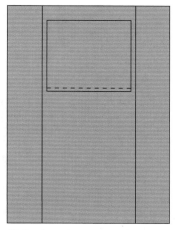

(1) Pocket placement

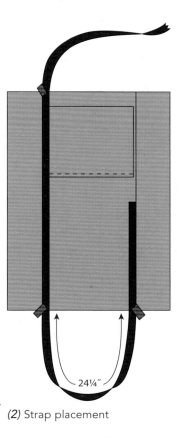

(2) Strap placement

Makeup Bag

Finished bag: 7˝ wide × 4¾˝ high × 1˝ deep

I know it's called a makeup bag, but really, you can use it for anything you like—use it to hold jewelry when you're traveling; stash some cash and use it as a little purse; keep your business cards, loyalty cards, hair clips…well, I think you get the idea.

MATERIALS AND SUPPLIES

- **kraft•tex (white):** 9″ × 14″ (This piece is large and will be cut after dyeing. You can adjust the size as you wish.)

- **Circle template or small plate to trace** that fits your kraft•tex piece

- **Image to transfer**

- **Lesley Riley's TAP Transfer Artist Paper:** 1 sheet

- **Dye** (I used COLORHUE Instant-Set Dye in turquoise.)

- **Zipper:** 12″ (or longer) in coordinating color

- **Hot water and rubber gloves**

- **Dorland's Wax Medium** (*optional*)

Artist:
Marie Z. Johansen

Marie Z. Johansen began her artistic life as a weaver. In 1976, however, she began a lifelong love affair with quilting (both traditional and art quilts). She once told a friend she didn't think she'd ever enjoy mixed-media art, but ironically mixed-media art has since come to dominate her creative life. Asking "What if…?" has led to almost daily "artventures" and creative explorations. Marie's art has been featured at International Quilt Festival in Houston, Texas, and her work has appeared in several books and magazines.

Company: *Musing Crow Designs*
Website:
www.musingcrowdesigns.com

INSTRUCTIONS

Refer to All about kraft•tex (page 4) for basic information.

1. Soak the piece of kraft•tex in *very* hot water for about 5–10 minutes. Have your dye colors selected and ready to go. I like COLORHUE dyes for this because they require no mixing and are ready to go.

2. Wearing rubber gloves, "torture" the kraft•tex by balling, wrapping, twisting, and otherwise manipulating it. You are aiming to create texture.

3. Leave the kraft•tex twisted up on a waterproof surface. Slowly and gently pour color onto the kraft•tex. You can choose how much of the surface to cover (I left a lot of background plain). If you are using more than one color, make certain that the colors mix and blend in some areas.

4. Let the color absorb into the kraft•tex (it will be absorbed quickly). When the color is stable, smooth the kraft•tex open and lay it flat. Let it dry thoroughly. It should show texture but retain its original dimensions. You can also put the kraft•tex in the dryer, but I find the texture stays better if I let it dry by itself.

5. When the kraft•tex is dry, cut it to 7½˝ × 10½˝ and fold the piece in half lengthwise, matching the top edges. Place the circle template or a small plate on the top edges. Draw along the curve shape. In general, it's best to choose a plate or circle that provides a *gentle curve for the top edge* of the bag. Cut along the curved line for both upper edges.

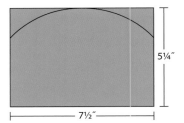

Draw and cut curve.

6. Follow the manufacturer's instructions to transfer your image onto the TAP. Remember that you need to take into account a ¼˝ seam allowance and that the transferred image will be mirrored. If you want the image to face a particular direction or if it has words, remember to mirror the image (or "flip horizontal") with your imaging software before printing.

7. Choose where on the bag to place the image; then transfer the image to the kraft•tex.

8. Sew the zipper to the curved edge of the bag using your favorite method. There is no need to turn under the edge of the kraft•tex. I sewed the zipper in with 2 rows of topstitching along each side.

Note

A word of caution when backstitching on kraft•tex: Do not sew any seam more than once—sewing perforates the kraft•tex. The holes that sewing makes are permanent. Be sure to use as small a needle as possible (I used a 90/14 topstitch needle with 12-weight thread).

9. Sew the sides of the bag together.

10. Gently turn the bag inside out. Finger-press the side seams flat, matching the seam to the fold on the bottom of the bag. Create a gusset by drawing a line ½″ from the tip of the corner of the bag and sewing along that line.

Either place a dab of glue at the ends or backstitch to ensure that the stitching will not pull out.

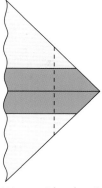

Wrong side, showing how to stitch boxed corner

11. Turn the bag right side out, gently pushing the corners out.

12. *Optional:* Gently rub Dorland's Wax Medium (see Resources, page 119) into the kraft•tex with a soft cloth and buff to a light shine. The wax also provides the bag with a bit of water resistance.

13. *Optional:* Add a bit of colorful yarn or beads to the zipper tab for a zipper pull.

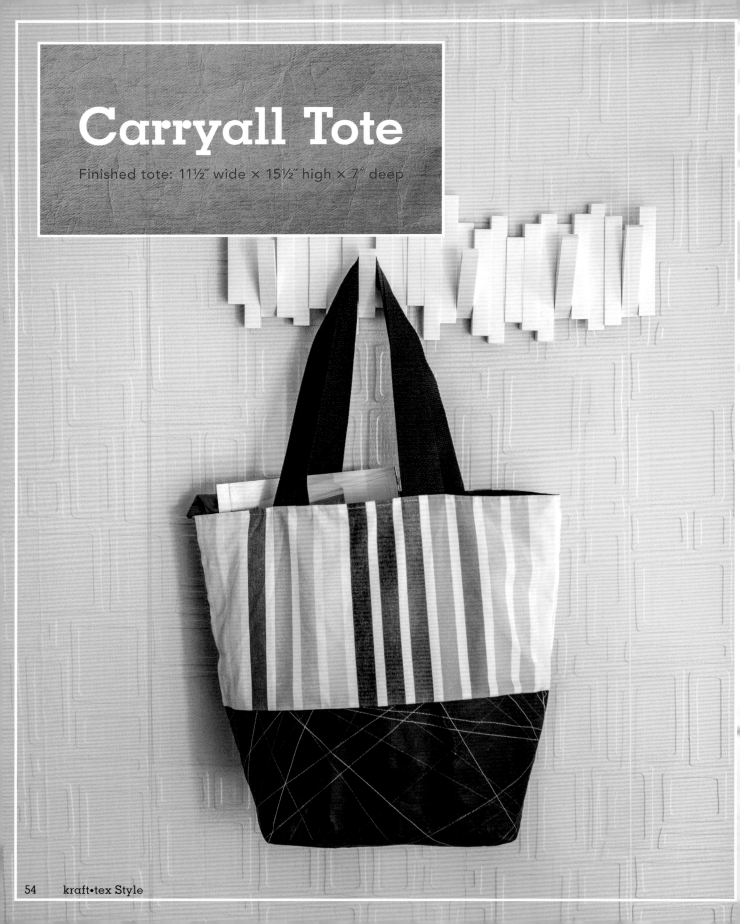

Carryall Tote

Finished tote: 11½˝ wide × 15½˝ high × 7˝ deep

You can never have too many bags. This one is the perfect size for just about any outing, from grocery shopping to camping. You will not be disappointed with this great tote. As a bonus, it's reversible.

MATERIALS AND SUPPLIES

- **Heavyweight canvas or duck cloth:** ⅝ yard
- **kraft•tex:** ⅝ yard
- **Print fabric:** ⅜ yard (If you are using quilting cotton, stabilize the fabric with a woven fusible interfacing, such as Shape-Flex.)
- **Cotton webbing, 1½˝ or 2˝ wide:** 48˝
- **80/12 Sharp needle**
- **Rotary cutter and cutting mat**

CUTTING

Canvas
- Cut 1 rectangle 19˝ × 39˝.

kraft•tex
- Cut 1 rectangle 19˝ × 20½˝.

Print fabric
- Cut 2 pieces 9¾˝ × 19˝.

Artist:
Jen Carlton Bailly

See Jen's profile in Tech Stand (page 34).

INSTRUCTIONS

Refer to All about kraft•tex (page 4) for basic information.

Note: All seam allowances are ¼″ unless otherwise noted.

1. Using a decorative stitch or straight lines, sew a design on the piece of kraft•tex. This will become the bottom half of the bag.

2. Sew a print fabric piece to the kraft•tex, with right sides together, along the 19″ side. This forms the side of the bag. Repeat, sewing the second fabric piece to the other 19″ side of the kraft•tex.

3. Fold this bag piece in half crosswise, with right sides together and matching the seams. Sew the 2 side seams to form the exterior of the bag.

4. Pinch the bottom side of the bag into a triangle, matching the side seam to the bottom center crease. Measure 3½″ from the top point of this triangle. Draw a line and stitch across. Repeat on the other bottom side. Trim off the corner triangles, leaving a ¼″ seam allowance. Turn the bag right side out.

⊢——— 3½″ ———⊣

Stitch across to create boxed corner.

5. Repeat Steps 3 and 4 using the canvas to make the interior of the bag, except leave the interior bag inside out.

6. Cut the webbing into 2 equal pieces for the handles. Place the ends of a strap on the top edge of the bag, 5″ from each side seam and hanging on the outside of the bag. Secure the strap with several lines of stitching ¼″ from the edge. Repeat for the second strap on the other side.

Strap placement

7. Insert the bag exterior into the interior bag, with right sides together. Pin the top of the bag and sew across the top using a ½″ seam allowance. Leave a 4″ opening on a side of the bag for turning.

8. Turn the bag right side out through the opening. Press the top of the bag flat. Topstitch ¼″ from the edge all the way around the bag.

Tri-Color Tote

Finished tote: 13½″ wide × 13″ high × 4″ deep

Artist:

Betsy La Honta

See Betsy's profile in Snowflake Wallhanging (page 22).

This handsome tote may be the only tote you need in your life—use it for shopping, picnicking, or toting your essentials for work or play.

MATERIALS AND SUPPLIES

- **kraft•tex:** 1 roll each of natural, black, and white
- **Fabric:** ¼ yard for handles
- **Purse hardware:** 4 rectangular metal rings (1½˝ × 1˝)
- **Binder or quilting clips**

CUTTING

kraft•tex (natural)

- Cut 2 pieces 4½˝ × 18˝ for body of tote.
- Cut 2 pieces ¾˝ × 25˝ for handles.
- Cut 4 pieces 1¼˝ × 4˝ for handle tabs.

kraft•tex (white)

- Cut 2 pieces 4½˝ × 18˝ for body of tote.

kraft•tex (black)

- Cut 2 pieces 8˝ × 18˝ for body of tote.
- Cut 1 or 2 pieces 3˝ × 4½˝ for pocket(s).

Fabric

- Cut 2 pieces 2˝ × 25˝ for handles.

INSTRUCTIONS

Refer to All about kraft•tex (page 4) for basic information.

Note: Seam allowances are ½˝ unless otherwise noted.

Tote Bag

1. Place a long edge of the natural 4½˝ × 18˝ kraft•tex strip overlapping the corresponding white strip by ½˝. Topstitch about 1/16˝ from the edge of the natural strip to hold together the 2 strips. Topstitch again ¼˝ from the first line of stitching.

2. Place the other long edge of the natural kraft•tex strip overlapping the black strip ½˝ and sew together as in Step 1.

3. Repeat Steps 1 and 2 for the other set of bag strips.

4. Topstitch along the top edge of both white pieces, 1/16˝ and ¼˝ down from the edge, to finish the upper edge of the tote.

5. Center the pocket(s) on the tan strip(s). Stitch around the pocket 1/8˝ from the edge, leaving the top open.

Pocket placement

Handles

1. Fold 1 fabric 2˝ × 25˝ piece in half lengthwise, wrong sides together, and press lightly. Unfold and fold each long edge to the center and press again, ironing out the first center fold. You should now have a fabric strip 1˝ × 25˝.

2. Place the ¾˝ × 25˝ kraft•tex strip on the folded fabric strip, covering the raw edges.

Be sure the kraft•tex is centered along the length; then use binder clips or quilting clips to hold it in place. Topstitch along one long edge of the kraft•tex strip and then along the other.

3. Repeat Steps 1 and 2 to make the second handle.

4. Thread an end of a handle through the square ring, turn under the raw edge ½˝, and then sew the end to the handle by topstitching a small rectangle to secure the end.

Attach strap to ring.

Handle Tabs

1. Fold a 1¼˝ × 4˝ piece of natural kraft•tex in half crosswise. Slide a rectangular metal ring onto the kraft•tex strip and sew across the strip approximately ½˝ down from the folded edge to hold the ring in place.

2. Place the tab and ring on the white strip of the kraft•tex tote body, butted next to the natural-colored strip and lined up with the outer edge of the pocket. Topstitch a square on the tab to secure it to the tote.

3. Repeat Steps 1 and 2 with the other 3 tabs.

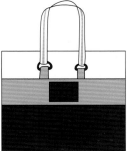

Strap placement

Assembly

1. Align the assembled body pieces, right sides together, making sure to match up the seams between the different colors of kraft•tex. Clip together and sew the sides and bottom.

2. To make the boxed bottom corners, pinch in a bottom and a side seam on one side, match the seams, and clip to hold closed, pushing the side and bottom seam allowances in opposite directions. Draw a line across the bottom of the corner triangle, approximately 2″ from the point of the triangle. Sew along the line, backstitching at the start and finish, to make the corner. Trim the triangle off, leaving a ½″ seam allowance.

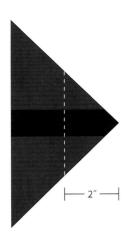

Sew boxed corner.

3. Repeat Step 2 to create the other corner.

4. Turn the tote right side out and load it up.

Zippered Pouch

Finished pouch: 10" × 6½"

What makes cows happy? Faux leather! Use this zippered pouch as an everyday organizer to keep essentials together, store receipts in your purse, or keep track of all your loyalty cards. Not partial to cows? Decorate and embellish it with your favorite motifs.

MATERIALS AND SUPPLIES

- **kraft•tex (natural):** ½ yard
- **Quilting-weight cotton fabric:** ⅓ yard or 1 fat quarter
- **Embroidery floss:** less than 1 skein each of 4 colors (I used dark brown, black, cream, and pale green.)
- **8˝ zipper**
- **Jump ring**
- **Self-healing cutting mat, rotary cutter, and rulers**
- **Carbon or graphite transfer paper** to transfer embroidery design
- **Zipper foot**
- **Embroidery needle**
- **Craft knife,** such as an X-ACTO (*optional*)
- **Paper clips or masking tape**
- **Pliers**

CUTTING

Note: If you want the look of textured leather, wash and dry the kraft•tex before cutting.

kraft•tex
- Cut 2 rectangles 6½˝ × 10˝ for clutch front and back.
- Cut 2 strips ¼˝ × 10˝ for zipper pull.

Quilting-weight cotton fabric
- Cut 1 rectangle 10˝ × 11˝ for bag lining.

INSTRUCTIONS

Refer to All about kraft•tex (page 4) for basic information.

Fabric Preparation and Embroidery

1. Place the front exterior kraft•tex piece horizontally on a flat surface. With a pencil, lightly draw a ½˝ × 7½˝ horizontal rectangle 1¼˝ from the top edge and each side of the kraft•tex.

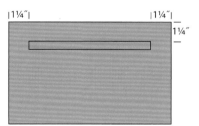

Draw rectangle.

2. Using carbon or graphite transfer paper, transfer the embroidery pattern (page 65) to the front exterior kraft•tex piece so that the design is centered horizontally and approximately 1¼˝ from the bottom.

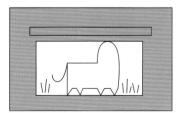

Transfer embroidery design.

3. Embroider the design on the kraft•tex piece using the stitch and color guide. Because of the stiffness of the kraft•tex, you will not need an embroidery hoop. It can be helpful to pre-poke the stitch holes prior to actually embroidering.

Lines: backstitch
Hair: seed stitch
Nostrils: french knots

Stitch and color guide

4. With scissors or a craft knife and ruler, cut out the rectangle you drew in Step 1.

Attaching the Zipper and Lining

1. With right sides up, place the embroidered kraft•tex opening over the closed zipper, centering the zipper vertically within the opening. Hold the zipper in place, using paper clips or masking tape, and sew the zipper to the kraft•tex, along only the short edges of the opening, with a ¹⁄₁₆˝ seam allowance.

Sew along short edges.

2. Flip the piece over so that it is wrong side up and horizontal, with the zipper toward the top. With the lining fabric wrong side up, place the bottom 10″ edge of the lining fabric along the bottom edge of the zipper. Line up the long sides of the lining with the sides of the kraft•tex. Pin the bottom edges of the zipper and lining. *Do not pin the kraft•tex.* Using paper clips, clip the kraft•tex to the lining.

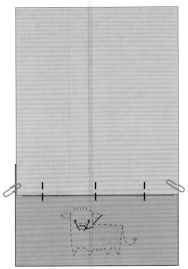

Pin lining to zipper; paper clip lining to kraft•tex.

3. Flip the piece so that the right sides are facing up. Using a zipper foot and a 1/16″ seam allowance, sew through the kraft•tex, zipper, and lining along the bottom edge of the opening only. Flip the pieces again so the wrong sides are facing up. Press the lining toward the bottom of the piece.

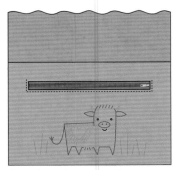

Sew along bottom edge.

4. The lining should now be right side up, with the wrong side of the kraft•tex and zipper toward the top. Fold the lining, bringing the bottom edge of the lining up to the top edge of the zipper. Pin the edge of the lining and zipper. Clip the kraft•tex to the lining as in Step 2.

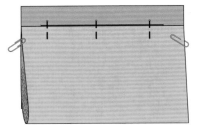

Pin lining to top zipper edge.

5. Flip over the piece. Sew along the top edge of the opening using a 1/16″ seam allowance, making sure the excess lining fabric is moved out of the way.

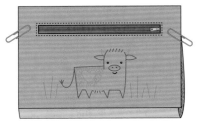

Sew along top edge.

6. Flip the piece over so the wrong side of the lining is facing up. Place your hands in the lining "tube" and finger-press the seam up and away from the zipper. Adjust the lining tube so that, when flattened, the lining is centered vertically on the kraft•tex. The top fold is 3/4″ and the bottom fold is 4 1/4″ from the zipper seams. Press flat.

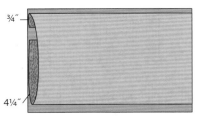

Center and press lining "tube."

7. Pin the side seams of the lining and sew with a ¼˝ seam allowance. Avoid pinning or sewing the kraft•tex. Trim the lining seam allowance to ⅛˝. Set aside.

Assembling the Case

1. Open the zipper and pull the lining through to the front. This will keep the lining out of the way for the next steps.

2. Use paper clips to hold both exterior kraft•tex pieces together, wrong sides together, along the top edge and right side only.

3. Sew around the entire edge of the exterior pieces with a ¼˝ seam allowance. Reinsert the lining.

Finishing

Thread the ¼˝ × 10˝ strips through the jump ring and fold them in half. Sew a few small stitches through all 4 layers of the zipper pull near the jump ring. Use pliers to open the jump ring by twisting the ends sideways and slip it through the hole in the zipper. Close the jump ring with the pliers.

Embroidery Pattern

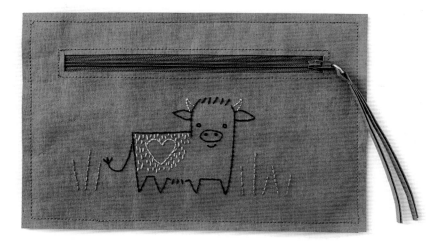

Bike Bag

Finished bag: 6⅜″ wide × 5¾″ high × 2½″ deep

If you need a bike bag, kraft•tex is the perfect material to use. My best friend bikes home from work each day, and this bag carries all her necessities. It is also versatile enough to tie around your waist when your destination has been reached.

MATERIALS AND SUPPLIES

- **kraft•tex:** ½ yard (½ package or ½ yard off the bolt)
- **Cotton fabric:** ¼ yard
- **Contrasting cotton fabric:** ⅛ yard (*optional*)
- **Large dog leash clasp (swivel latch):** 1¼˝ (*optional, for inner key clip*)
- **Binding clips** (*optional*)

CUTTING

kraft•tex
- Cut 1 piece 6½˝ × 7˝ for back.
- Cut 2 pieces 6˝ × 7˝ for front and flap.
- Cut 1 piece 3˝ × 16˝ for side.
- Cut 5 pieces 1˝ × 3˝ for outer pulls.
- Cut 8 pieces ⅛˝ × 18˝ for ties.

Cotton fabric
- Cut 1 piece 6½˝ × 7˝ for lining back.
- Cut 2 pieces 6˝ × 7˝ for lining front and flap.
- Cut 1 piece 3˝ × 16˝ for lining sides.

Contrasting cotton fabric
- Cut 1 piece 7˝ × 8˝ for inner pocket.
- Cut 1 piece 3˝ × 4˝ for inner pull for dog leash clasp.

Artist:
Michelle Jensen

Michelle Jensen established Mixi Heart in 2012. She lives in Utah, where she works as a pattern designer and longarm quilter. Most days you can find her in her sewing room making bags, quilting, or piecing with friends. She loves the fabric industry and hopes you enjoy her little heartfelt contribution.

Company: *Mixi Heart*
Website: *mixiheart.com*

INSTRUCTIONS

Refer to All about kraft•tex (page 4) for basic information.

Note: Seam allowances are ¼˝ unless otherwise noted.

The Lining

1. Round both corners on a 7˝ side of the 6½˝ × 7˝ and 6˝ × 7˝ fabric pieces using the rounding tool pattern (page 70).

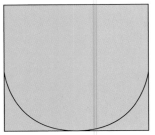

Round corners.

2. Create the pocket by folding the 7˝ × 8˝ pocket piece in half crosswise with wrong sides together. Topstitch the top of the pocket ¼˝ from the folded edge. Round the bottom corners of the pocket. Place the pocket on top of a 6½˝ × 7˝ back piece. Clip or pin the pocket in place.

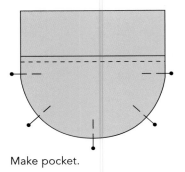

Make pocket.

3. Fold the 3˝ × 4˝ strip in half lengthwise with right sides together. Sew along the raw edge of the 4˝ side. Turn right side out, center the seam, and press flat. Topstitch ¼˝ from the folded edges.

4. Fold the strip in half crosswise and slip the dog leash clasp on if you are using one. Clip or pin this piece in place 1˝ from the left top edge of the back piece and stitch ⅛˝ from the edge.

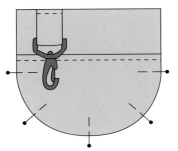

Add key clip tab.

5. Place a 6˝ × 7˝ flap piece on top of the back piece, right sides together. Sew along the top edge. Press the seam toward the back and set aside.

6. Clip or pin the 3˝ × 16˝ side strip to the sides and around the curved bottom of the 7˝ × 6˝ front piece, right sides together. (*Note: Gently ease into the rounded corners.*) Sew along the outer edge, leaving a 3˝ hole for turning at the bottom. Trim the side piece even with the top edge of the front if necessary.

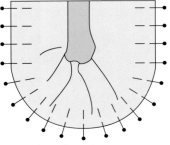

Sew side to front.

7. Clip the other side of the 3˝ × 16˝ strip to the back piece, right sides together. Sew along the outer edge. Leave the lining wrong side out and set aside.

Outer Body

1. Before beginning to sew, round both corners on a 7˝ side of the 6½˝ × 7˝ and 6˝ × 7˝ pieces using the rounding tool (page 70).

2. To add embroidery, use the circle pattern (page 70) to trace the shape onto the front of the bag flap and bag body. Backstitch with embroidery floss to stitch your design. My stitches were about ⅛˝–³⁄₁₆˝ apart.

3. To make the outer ties, cut 2 of the 8 ties in half to create a total of 4 ties 9˝ long and 6 ties 18˝ long. Fold the 1˝ × 3˝ strips in half crosswise. Insert 2 ties into the fold of each 1˝ × 3˝ strip. Sew around the edge of the pulls ¼˝ from the edges, creating an inner stitched square to encase the tie ends.

4. Clip a long tie to the left top of the 6½˝ × 7˝ back body piece, 1˝ from the side and ¾˝ over the edge. (*Note: The long ties should be pointing toward the rounded side.*) Clip another long tie to the top right of the back outer body, 1˝ out from the side and ¾˝ over the edge. Clip the last long tie to the left side of the back piece, 1˝ down from the top and ¾˝ over the edge. Clip a short tie centered on the rounded side of a 6˝ × 7˝ flap piece, also ¾˝ over the edge. (*Note: The short ties should be pointing away from the rounded side.*) Clip the remaining short tie centered ¾˝ from the rounded side of the front piece. Stitch this last tie to the front, following the previous stitching.

5. Stitch together the flap (the one with the tie on the edge) and the back pieces along the top edge. Press the seam toward the flap and reinforce the seam with zigzag stitching along the edge. Set aside.

6. Clip the 3˝ × 16˝ strip to the front piece. (*Note: Gently ease into the rounded corners.*) Sew along the outer edge and trim the sides even with the top of the front if necessary. Clip the other side of the 3˝ × 16˝ strip to the back piece. Sew along the outer edge. Turn the outer bag right side out.

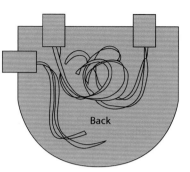

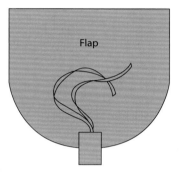

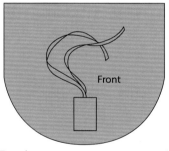

Tie placement

Final Combination

1. Slide the outer bag inside the lining. Clip in place.

2. Sew along the top edge and the flap.

3. Turn right side out through the turning hole. Close the turning hole in the inner lining by topstitching ⅛″ from the edge. Push the lining down inside the outer body. Topstitch ⅛″ from the edge along the top of the flap and around the top edge of the bag opening.

You have just completed your bag. Tie it to your bike and go for a ride!

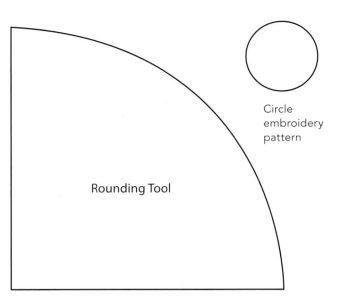

Rounding Tool

Circle embroidery pattern

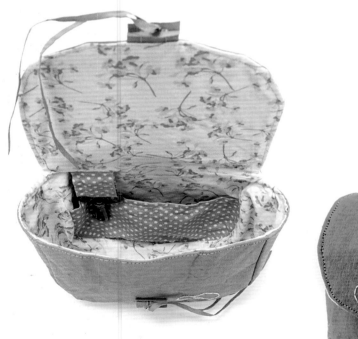

Accessorize

Wallet

Finished wallet: 8¾″ × 4″

I love being able to make my own accessories. With kraft•tex you can make just about any that you want. With fabric as the outer layer, you can coordinate this wallet with anything… and everything.

MATERIALS AND SUPPLIES

- **kraft•tex:** ½ yard
- **Quilting-weight cotton fabric:** 12″ × 12″
- **Fusible webbing:** 2 sheets (I used Steam-A-Seam.)
- **6″ zipper**
- **Topstitching thread** to match kraft•tex color
- **Leather needle** for sewing machine
- **Heavy-duty jeans snap press:** 1
- **Paper-backed double-sided tape,** ¼″ wide
- **Hera marker** (or you can carefully use a tailor's awl)
- **Small bulldog clips or quilting clips**
- **Rotary cutter, quilting ruler, and cutting mat**
- **Point cutter, utility blade, or box cutter**
- **Hammer**
- **Appliqué mat or baking parchment** (You can also use Silicone Release Paper by C&T Publishing.)
- **Hole punch**
- **Clear-drying craft glue**

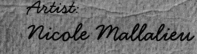

Artist:
Nicole Mallalieu

Nicole Mallalieu has been sewing obsessively since the age of three. She has a fashion degree and has enjoyed fifteen years in the fashion and craft industries of Australia, England, and Ireland, specializing mostly in handcrafted hats and bags for the boutique market. In 2003, she began Nicole Mallalieu Design (which was rebranded YOU SEW GIRL! in 2011), designing bag and purse patterns and teaching bag making. Over the last six years, she's been an avid craft blogger and has become popular online in the United States. She is the author of *The Better Bag Maker*, published by Stash Books. She lives in Melbourne, Australia.

Company: *YOU SEW GIRL!*
Website: *nicolemdesign.com.au*

CUTTING

kraft•tex

The width of each piece is measured across the 19″ width of the kraft•tex. Grain is important for this project.

- Cut 2 pieces 8⅝″ × 8″ for outside and pocket base.

- Cut 1 piece 8⅝″ × 6¼″ for zipper pocket.

- Cut 1 piece 8⅝″ × 2½″ for card pocket.

- Cut 1 piece 8⅝″ × 2⅞″ for card pocket.

- Cut 1 piece 8⅝″ × 3¼″ for card pocket.

- Cut 2 pieces 1½″ × 4″ for closure tab.

Cotton fabric

- Cut 1 piece 10⅛″ × 9½″.

Fusible webbing

- Cut 1 piece 10⅛″ × 9½″. (You can piece the webbing together, if necessary, to fit the fabric.)

- Cut 1 piece 1½″ × 4″.

INSTRUCTIONS

Refer to All about kraft•tex (page 4) for basic information.

Preparing the Pieces

Note: I consider the smoother side of kraft•tex the "right" side.

1. Fuse the 2 closure tab pieces wrong sides together with fusible web; then cut a rectangle 1¼″ × 3⅝″ for the closure tab.

2. Turn the zipper pocket piece wrong side up and mark a line through the center, across the width (3⅛″ from the top and bottom). Mark parallel lines ³⁄₁₆″ from each side of this line. Draw a line across the ends of these lines, 1¼″ in from each of the side edges.

Draw zipper box.

3. Using a ruler and rotary cutter along the long edges and a point cutter at the short ends, cut out the rectangular shape in the center of the kraft•tex.

4. On the right side of the zipper pocket piece, use a Hera marker to draw a stitching line around the rectangle a scant ⅛″ from the cut edge.

5. With the right side of the kraft•tex facing up, place the 3 pocket pieces of kraft•tex on top of each other—the largest at the bottom and the smallest at the top. Align the pieces along a long edge and at the short ends.

6. Use a Hera marker and ruler to mark the stitch lines 4¼″ from each of the short ends across all 3 layers. These will become the card pockets of the wallet.

Mark center divider of pockets.

Sewing the Card Pockets

1. With the right side of the kraft•tex facing up, place the 3 card pocket pieces on the pocket base. Align the long edges of the smaller pieces along a long edge of the pocket base and use bulldog clips or quilting clips to hold all the pieces firmly together.

2. Change your stitch length to a scant ⅛″ and thread the machine with topstitching thread. Following the Hera marker lines, stitch through all the layers, beginning a generous ⅛″ from the outer edge and going toward the top edge of the longest pocket piece. Stitch a U-turn; then stitch back down to ⅛″ from the outer edge. Do not backstitch. Pull the threads through to the wrong side of the pocket base and tie them together securely. Trim off the excess thread.

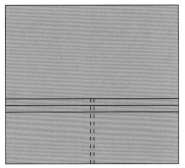

Sew pockets to pocket base.

Sewing the Zippered Pocket

1. On the wrong side of the zipper pocket piece, stick double-sided tape parallel to and a scant ⅛″ away from each of the long edges of the cutout rectangle. Remove the backing paper from the tape.

2. Position the zipper right side up beneath the cutout rectangle, making sure it is centered; then stick it to the back of the kraft•tex.

3. Stitch the zipper to the kraft•tex, following the Hera marker stitch line around the rectangle. Pull all the threads to the wrong side, tie them securely, and trim off the excess.

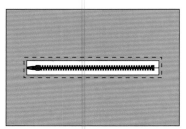

Stitch zipper in place.

4. Fold the rectangle to match the 2 long edges, with the zipper along the fold line. Use double-sided tape, starting ¼″ in from the edge, to hold the edges together.

5. Place the zippered pocket on the pocket base on the end opposite the card pockets. With the zipper toward the middle, align the outer edges of the zipper pocket with the base piece. Use double-sided tape, starting ¼″ in from the edge, to hold the zipper pocket to the pocket base.

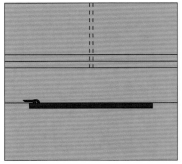

Add zipper pocket to pocket base.

Finishing the Inner Pockets

1. On the right side of all the pockets and base, use a Hera marker and ruler to mark a stitch line a full ½″ from the outer edges of the pocket base.

2. Stitch along the Hera marker line to hold all the layers together. Pull the threads to the back; then tie and trim the excess thread.

3. Using a quilting ruler and rotary cutter, trim the edge ⅜″ from the stitching, making all the edges neat and flush.

Making the Outer Wallet

1. Following the manufacturer's directions for your fusible web, fuse the web to the wrong side of the fabric piece and place it fusible side up.

2. Place the outside piece of kraft•tex in the center of the fabric piece so that there is an even ¾″ of fabric visible all the way around the kraft•tex. With the 2 pieces in this position and the kraft•tex on top, place an appliqué pressing sheet or a sheet of Silicone Release Paper (see Resources, page 119) over the top and press with a hot iron to fuse the 2 layers together. Turn over and press from the right side of the fabric; allow it to cool before removing it from the pressing sheet.

3. Slip the appliqué pressing sheet (or use Silicone Release Paper) under this unit to protect the ironing board. Using the edges of the kraft•tex as a fold line, turn under the fabric on the 2 side edges and press from the fabric side of the kraft•tex to make a crease. Do not press and fuse the fabric at the corners.

4. Turn to the wrong side and trim the folded corners off at a diagonal, 1½″ down the edge of the fabric. Press carefully to fuse the fabric to the kraft•tex without touching your iron to the exposed fusible web.

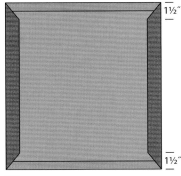

1½″

1½″

Trim corners.

5. Fold each corner point ½″ toward the wrong side of the fabric and press into place with the tip of the iron.

½″

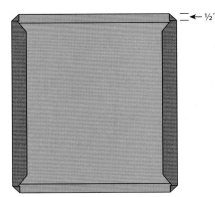

Fold and fuse corners.

6. Using the edges of the kraft•tex as a fold line again, fold the fabric on the other 2 edges over and press to fuse the fabric to the kraft•tex.

7. On a long edge of the outside piece, mark the snap placement 1″ from the edge and in the middle of the wallet width (4⅜″ from each end). Punch or poke a hole at this point and insert the bottom half of a snap press.

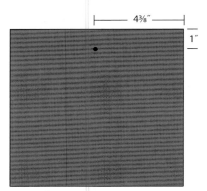

Snap placement

Making the Closure Tab

1. Use a Hera marker and ruler to mark a stitch line all around the tab, ⅛″ in from the edge.

2. Beginning at a short end of the tab, stitch on the line. Pull the threads to the back, tie them together, and trim off the excess.

3. With a Hera marker, draw a stitch line ⅝″ from where you began stitching. On the short end opposite where you began stitching, mark the snap placement centered ⅞″ from the edge.

Stitching and snap placement

4. Punch a hole through the placement mark and insert the top half of the snap.

5. Measure and mark the tab placement 1⅝″ from the edge on the outer wallet piece, centered along the edge that doesn't have the lower part of the snap.

6. Use double-sided tape to hold the last ¾″ of the tab in place on the wallet piece. Check that the snap on the tab aligns with the snap on the wallet and that it closes properly.

7. Following the stitches around the edge of the tab and the stitch line at the ⅝″ mark, stitch the tab into place on the wallet outside. Pull the threads to the wrong side of the outer wallet, tie them together, and trim off the excess.

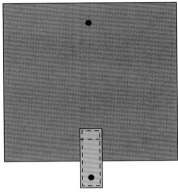

Stitching tab to wallet

Assembling the Wallet

1. Trace the pocket base onto a sheet of fusible web. Cut the webbing to size and follow the manufacturer's directions to fuse it to the wrong side of the pocket base.

2. Place the pocket base and the outer wallet piece wrong sides together, centering the base so that there is an even amount of the outer wallet visible all the way around it. The zipper pocket should be on the side that has the snap tab.

3. Using a steam iron (with lots of steam), press from both sides to fuse the 2 pieces together.

4. On the right side of the wallet, beginning at the point underneath the closure tab, stitch ¼″ from the edge to attach the outer layer to the inner layers. Pull the threads through to the outer side (underneath the tab), tie them together, and trim off the excess thread. Use a spot of clear-drying craft glue on the knotted thread ends to secure the knot.

Snap your wallet closed and admire your handiwork!

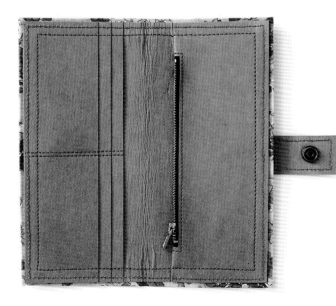

Beaded Feather Earrings

Finished earrings: 5⁄8″ × 1 7⁄8″

Light and feathery with just a smidge of pearly glimmer, these earrings are perfect for any outfit—from your dressiest frock to a simple T-shirt and jeans.

MATERIALS AND SUPPLIES

- **kraft•tex:** scraps
- **Upholstery thread**
- **Beading needles**
- **Glass tube beads, 2mm**
- **Craft paint** (I used pale blue, ocean blue, silver, and clear pearlescent.)
- **Earring hooks**
- **1mm hole punch or large needle**
- **Chain-nose pliers**
- **Craft glue**

Artist:
Maryellen Kim

Maryellen Kim lives in Virginia with her husband, three kids, and a very fuzzy cat. Her designs are a reflection of the two main joys of her life: family and creativity. A self-proclaimed supply hoarder, Maryellen has never met a craft medium she didn't love. Her days are spent running the Twist Style jewelry design and production studio; running kids around; and managing her brick-and-mortar storefront, Handmade Happiness Boutique. If she's not hanging out in the studio making stuff, she's probably at home in her secret hideout perusing Pinterest.

Company: *Twist Style*
Website: *twiststyle.com, facebook.com/twiststyle*
Instagram and Twitter: *@twiststyle*

INSTRUCTIONS

Refer to All about kraft•tex (page 4) for basic information.

1. Photocopy or trace the feather pattern (below) and cut it out to make a template. Use the template to cut 2 feathers from the kraft•tex.

2. Paint both sides of the kraft•tex pale blue. When the base paint is dry, dab on ocean blue paint to create a feathered look. Next, paint the edges and tips silver.

When all is dry, lightly brush each entire feather with clear pearlescent paint. Let this dry as well.

3. Punch 11 holes about ⅛″ apart down the center of each feather quill.

4. Thread a needle with 16″ of upholstery thread and knot the end. Pass the needle through the first hole at the top of a feather quill. Add 1 tube bead before passing the needle through the second hole. Add the second bead (the first for the "back" side of the feather) before passing the thread through the third hole. Continue sewing beads on by adding

1 bead before each stitch. When you get to the tip of the feather, you will have 5 beads on each side of the feather. Add another bead and go back through the tenth hole, continuing back to the top to sew the remaining beads.

Adding beads

5. Repeat Step 4 for the second earring.

6. Tie off the thread and add a tiny dab of glue to keep the stitches from pulling out.

7. Attach an earring hook in the first hole at the top of each quill using pliers, making sure to turn a feather over so you have a mirror-imaged set.

You're now ready to dress up your favorite outfit.

Feather pattern

Super Fussy Frame Necklace

Finished necklace: 20˝–21˝ | Finished frame: 1⅝˝ × 1⅞˝

Artist:

Roxane Cerda

Roxane Cerda sews, knits, and makes jewelry when she isn't up to her eyeballs with her day job as the acquisitions editor for Stash Books. Roxane lives in Indianapolis, Indiana.

These are so easy to make that you'll be making them for yourself and all your friends. Feature your favorite images or ephemera and change the style of the chain and you have endless variations.

MATERIALS AND SUPPLIES

- **kraft•tex in desired color:** 2″ × 4″ scrap
- **Fabric scraps**
- **Ready-to-wear necklace chain:** 18″ to 21″
- **Jump rings, 4mm:** 2 (Be sure these are small enough to fit through the links of your chosen chain.)
- **Fabric glue**
- **Small, stiff paintbrush**
- **Small, sharp craft scissors**
- **Flush cutters**
- **Chain-nose pliers**
- **Markers**
- **3mm hole punch**

CUTTING

Be sure to use small, sharp craft scissors to ensure that you cleanly capture the shape of the frame.

- Photocopy or trace the frame front and frame back patterns (page 86) and cut both templates.

- Use a pencil and the template to trace the frame back onto kraft•tex. Cut 1.

- Use a pencil and the template to trace the frame front onto kraft•tex. Cut 1. Cut out the center.

INSTRUCTIONS

Refer to All about kraft•tex (page 4) for basic information.

1. Using the frame front, audition your various fabric scraps to find the best art piece for the frame.

Audition fabrics.

2. Once you have decided on the art piece, carefully draw a 1¼˝ × 1½˝ rectangle around it. You can measure and cut a template for this step or just use a ruler. Double-check that the art piece is placed as you wish in the rectangle; then cut it out.

3. Place the frame front on the frame back and make sure the 2 shapes line up. Trim if needed. Once you have identified the top and bottom of each piece, set the frame front aside.

4. On the top of the frame back, paint the center space with a thin layer of fabric glue. Adhere the fabric scrap to the frame back.

Spread glue on back.

5. Paint glue onto the wrong side of the frame front, omitting the 2 upper corners of the frame.

Prepare to glue frame top.

6. Place the frame front carefully on top of the frame back and press down to adhere. Gently wipe away any excess glue.

7. Use markers to decorate the frame. Look to your fabric scrap for ideas on color and design.

8. Using the hole punch, place holes in the 2 upper corners of the frame. Be careful to get close enough to the edge to accommodate the jump ring but not so close to the edge that the kraft•tex is perforated.

Punch holes in upper corners.

9. Determine the center of the chain and then snip it in half using the flush cutters. Note which side of the chain should go on the left and which on the right, depending upon your dominant hand. Set aside.

10. Use the chain-nose pliers to open the jump rings. Always open jump rings by twisting the sides of the jump ring away from one another sideways. Do not pull them apart from the center.

right   wrong

Right and wrong way to open jump ring

11. Thread a jump ring through the hole in a corner of the frame. Next, thread the end of a side (right or left) of the chain through the jump ring. Double-check those sides so that the necklace is not backward! Using the chain-nose pliers, push the sides of the jump ring back together to connect one side of the chain to the frame. Repeat for the other side.

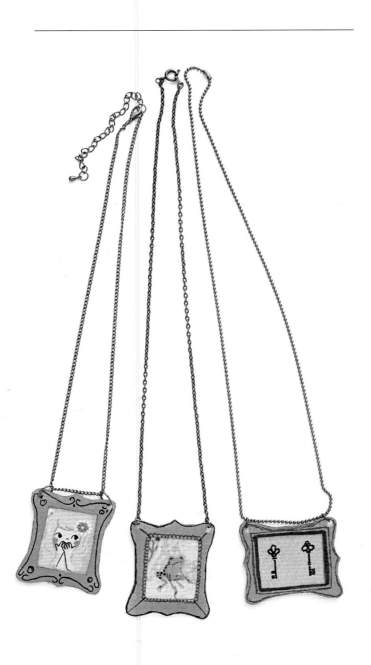

Easy Variation

If you wish, you can simplify the project by using oversized jump rings. Simply string the chain through the jump rings rather than attaching the chain to the ring.

Easy-peasy way

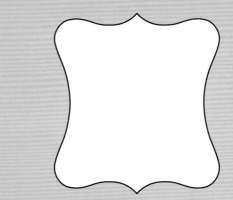

Frame back

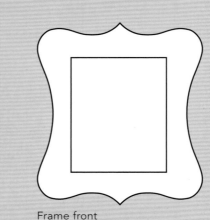

Frame front

For Fun

Vintage-Inspired Camera Strap

Finished strap: 2″ × 49½″

Combining fabric and kraft•tex allows you to make this vintage-inspired camera strap uniquely yours. Use your favorite fabric or scraps and you'll have a one-of-a-kind accessory for your camera.

MATERIALS AND SUPPLIES

Before you cut or sew, measure the width of the strap acceptor on your camera. The finished strap will need to fit through the channel on your camera.

- **kraft•tex:** 5″ × 19″
- **Fabric:** ⅛ yard
- **Featherweight interfacing:** ⅛ yard
- **Fusible fleece:** ⅛ yard
- **Fabric-marking pen**
- **Ruler**
- **Scoring pen**
- **Bone folder**
- **Clips** such as Wonder Clips (see Resources, page 119) or binder clips
- **Straight pins**
- **Jeans needle**
- **Coordinating thread**
- **Tube turning tool** (*optional*)
- **Camera strap hardware** with ½″ buckle (I sourced mine from an old camera strap that was no longer functional.)

CUTTING

kraft•tex
- Cut 2 pieces 2″ × 19″ for side straps.

Fabric
- Cut 2 pieces 2½″ × 21″ for neck strap.

Interfacing
- Cut 2 pieces 2½″ × 21″ for neck strap.

Fusible fleece
- Cut 1 piece 2″ × 15″ for neck strap.

Artist:

Heather Givans

Photo by Eric Lubrick

Sewing under the pseudonym Crimson Tate: Modern Quilter, Heather Givans is currently obsessed with creating quilts constructed from contemporary, modern, and repurposed vintage fabrics. Heather, who has degrees in art history, art education, and fine arts, taught high school art for ten years. Recently she has blazed a path along the Cultural Trail in downtown Indianapolis, where she owns a retail fabric store, teaches sewing lessons, and giggles with anyone who will giggle with her. She lives in an old Victorian house (with constant plumbing issues and an exorbitant amount of poison ivy) with her partner and two rat terriers.

Company: *Crimson Tate*
Website: *crimsontate.com*

INSTRUCTIONS

Refer to All about kraft•tex (page 4) for basic information.

Note: Seam allowances are ¼˝ unless otherwise noted.

Preparation

1. Wash the kraft•tex 2 or 3 times to soften the fibers. I washed mine in the washing machine with other laundry. Dry in the dryer or lay flat to dry.

2. Following the manufacturer's instructions, fuse the interfacing to the back of the fabric, taking care to use a pressing cloth.

3. Fold the ends of both fabric pieces in ¼˝ and press.

4. Find the lengthwise center of 1 interfaced strap by folding it in half and finger-pressing. Do the same to the fleece. Place the fleece on the interfaced side of the strap, matching the fold lines to center it and placing it 2¾˝ from both ends. Using a pressing cloth, fuse the fleece to the neck strap. Set aside.

Fleece placement

Tapering the Neck Strap

1. Along the side of the nonfleeced fabric strap, measure 3˝ in from the end, making a tick mark at the top and bottom. Along the end of the strap, measure and mark ¾˝ from the top and bottom. Repeat on the other end of the strap.

2. With a marking pen, connect a side point to an end point, resulting in a diagonal line. Repeat for the remaining 3 sets of points.

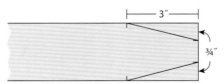

Mark diagonal lines.

Manhandling the kraft•tex

1. To create a cleaner, sharper crease, score the kraft•tex every ½˝ along the length of the piece, creating 3 score lines on each side strap.

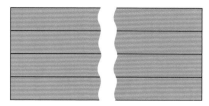

2. Fold in the 2 outer sections toward the center and press with a bone folder to flatten. Fold in half and press again. Repeat for the other strap.

Tip

Before folding, trim a scant ⅛˝ from both long edges to avoid extra bulk in the center.

3. On both straps, measure 14˝ from an end and make a mark to indicate where you will stop sewing.

Camera Strap Assembly

1. Using 4 or 5 clips for each side strap, clip along the open side to hold it closed.

Tips

• Increase your stitch length. It makes a prettier stitch.

• Backstitch at the beginning and end.

• A jeans needle easily handles kraft•tex. I'd recommend it on this portion of the project.

2. Starting at the end farthest from the 5˝ mark, topstitch ⅛˝ from the open edge of the side strap. Continue sewing to the 5˝ mark and use an *aggressive* backstitch at this mark. Sew both of the side straps. (Note: Be careful when backstitching—don't stitch directly over existing stitching; stitch slightly to one side or the other. Refer to Machine and Hand Sewing, page 6, as needed.)

3. Pin the neck strap fabric pieces right sides together.

4. Begin sewing at an end of the strap by sewing along the diagonal line (not ¼˝ away) and stop with your needle down ¼˝ from the side of the strap. Pivot; then sew along the length of the strap with a ¼˝ seam allowance until you reach the diagonal line at the end.

Pivot again and follow the diagonal line off the strap. Remember to backstitch at the beginning and end. Repeat for the other side of the strap.

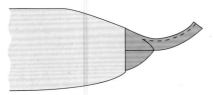

Sew neck strap.

5. Trim the excess fabric from the diagonal seam.

6. Turn the neck strap right side out using the tube turning tool or a large safety pin; then iron flat. Take care to iron well.

7. Thread the unsewn end of the side strap into the neck strap, opening and flattening the fold inside the neck strap. Clip it into place. Repeat with the other side strap on the opposite side.

Thread side strap into neck strap.

Finishing

1. Topstitch along the perimeter of the neck strap, pivoting at each turn, using an ⅛″ seam. Be sure to backstitch at the beginning and end and sew as close to the kraft•tex as your presser foot will allow.

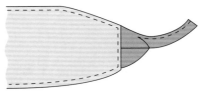

Topstitch neck strap.

Tip

Start the topstitching somewhere away from the center so as to be less noticeable. Again, increase the stitch length for a prettier stitch.

2. Thread the side straps through the hardware and your camera, adjusting the length to suit your preference.

Now go out and take great photos!

Ready-to-Travel Backgammon Board

Finished board: 10″ × 11½″ folded, 20″ × 11½″ unfolded

Artist:
Annabel Wrigley

Annabel Wrigley is a crafty Aussie mum living in the Virginia countryside. She owns Little Pincushion Studio, where she teaches sewing classes to a creative gang of sweet girls. (And a few clever boys!) She writes a blog by the same name, where she shares her daily inspirations, class adventures, and thrifty finds. She lives with her husband, Darren, and extra-crafty children, Ruby and Oliver. She is the author of *We Love to Sew* and *We Love to Sew—Bedrooms*, both published by FunStitch Studio.

Company: *Little Pincushion Studio*
Website: *littlepincushionstudio.com*

Backgammon is the perfect game to pass the time while traveling. The kraft•tex-embellished fabric board is so easy to roll and pack that you'll want to take it wherever you go.

MATERIALS AND SUPPLIES

Note: You will also need a pair of dice to play the game.

- **kraft•tex (white):** 10˝ × 10˝
- **kraft•tex (natural or black):** 10˝ × 10˝
- **Natural-colored utility cotton canvas fabric:** 1 fat quarter
- **Backing fabric:** 1 fat quarter
- **Binding and tie fabric:** ¼ yard
- **Cotton batting:** 12½˝ × 21˝
- **Water-soluble or erasable marking pen** (I used a Pilot FriXion pen.)
- **Water-soluble fabric gluestick**
- **Buttons:** 15 each of 2 colors, 1˝ diameter or smaller, for game pieces

CUTTING

kraft•tex
- Photocopy or trace the triangle pattern (page 96) and cut a template. Use the template to trace and cut 12 white triangles and 12 black or natural triangles of kraft•tex.

Cotton canvas
- Cut 1 piece 11½˝ × 20˝.

Backing fabric
- Cut 1 piece 12½˝ × 21˝.

Binding and tie fabric
- Cut 2 strips 3˝ × width of fabric.
- Cut 1 strip 3˝ × width of fabric.

INSTRUCTIONS

Refer to All about kraft•tex (page 4) for basic information.

1. Using the erasable marker, draw a line around the edge of the canvas fabric, ⅛″ from the edge. This will be the placement line for the triangles.

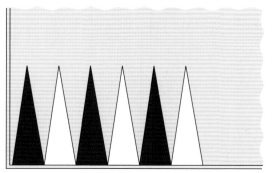

Draw edge lines.

2. Apply the fabric glue to the back of the first 3 white and 3 natural/black triangles. Starting at one corner, stick down the 6 triangles, alternating colors, with the bases on the line and touching each other.

Triangle placement

3. Using coordinating thread, sew close to the edge around each triangle. Make sure that you do not sew 2 of the same color side by side.

4. After you have sewn the first 6, start from the opposite side and attach the next 6 triangles in the same manner. There will be a gap in the middle of the board.

5. Now attach the remaining 12 triangles.

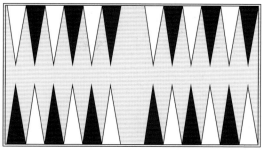

Board assembly diagram

6. Using the erasable pen, on the right side of the fabric, draw 6 lines down the length of the backing fabric to mark the quilting lines. The first line is 2½″ from the edge, and the next 5 are 1½″ apart.

7. Sandwich the batting and the backing fabric together and pin securely.

8. Sew down each of the lines. I prefer to use a walking foot for this, but a regular foot also works. Be sure to pin adequately. Remove the marking lines following the manufacturer's instructions.

9. Press the strip for the tie in half lengthwise; then fold in the short ends of the strip ¼″ and press. Then fold in each long edge to the center crease and press again.

10. Sew down both the sides and the ends of the strip, approximately ⅛″ from the edge.

11. Fold the backing piece in half crosswise to find the center. Mark this center point between the center 2 quilting lines. Place the tie across this mark, with the tie running lengthwise across the back piece. Machine stitch the tie in place at this center point.

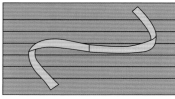

Tie placement

12. Place the board piece faceup on top of the batting side of the back piece and pin it in place. There should be ½″ extra on each side.

13. Sew around the edge just below the base of the triangles.

14. Trim around the edge of the game board top.

15. Sew the binding strips together diagonally at the short ends, right sides together, and press the entire strip in half, wrong sides together.

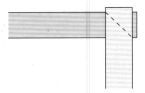

Piece binding diagonally.

16. Attach the binding to the front with a ⅜″ seam allowance; then fold the binding to the back and blindstitch all the way around.

Give the whole piece a good press, gather the buttons and dice, and you are ready to play!

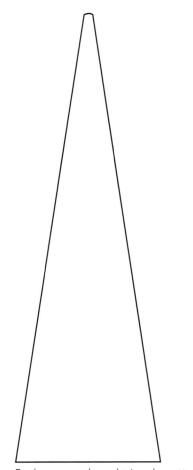

Backgammon board triangle pattern

Dolly and Wardrobe Play Set

Finished doll: 5⅛″ wide × 7¾″ high × ⅛″ deep
Finished clothing: approximately 4½″ × 4½″

Artist:

Karen LePage

Karen LePage is a gentle-living, hard-rocking, granola-geek-like, yoga-practicing, veggie-eating wife-mom-friend-sister-daughter-artist. She rides a motorcycle and has climbed mountains, both literally and figuratively. Karen cohosts Southeast Michigan Crafty Meetups every month, designs sewing patterns, teaches sewing classes, and volunteers in the Ann Arbor and Detroit crafty communities. She loves teaching almost as much as she loves learning.

Karen worked as a sewing pattern designer for kids' clothes at Patterns by Figgy's and co-wrote *Sewing for Boys*, a book of patterns to make a boy's complete wardrobe.

Company: *One Girl Circus*
Website: *onegirlcircus.com*

Take a cue from the pre–digital everything days with these sweet dolls and wardrobe. Mix and match the hair and clothes—or, better yet, let your kids help you decide.

MATERIALS AND SUPPLIES

- **kraft•tex:** 1 roll (19″ × 1½ yards)
- **Batting:** 5½″ × 8″ (I like Warm & Natural.)
- **Fusible web:** 1 package (I like Steam-A-Seam 2.)
- **Scraps of fabric** for clothing
- **Scraps of wool felt** for hair
- **³⁄₁₆″ hole punch**
- **Baker's twine or ⅛″-wide ribbon:** 1 yard for each set of clothes
- **Paint, markers, or colored pencils** for decorating doll's face
- **Scrap trim, decorative yarn, or beads** (*optional*)
- **Grommets/eyelets** to reinforce punch holes (*optional*)
- **Embroidery floss** (*optional*)

INSTRUCTIONS

Refer to All about kraft•tex (page 4) for basic information.

Making the Dolly

1. Photocopy or trace the doll pattern (page 101) and cut it out. Place it on top of the kraft•tex and trace it twice with a pencil. Cut out 2 dollies.

2. Trace the pattern onto batting. Cut the shape just inside the tracing marks so that the marks are cut away. The batting will be slightly smaller than the kraft•tex.

3. Embroider a face onto the dolly. Or you can paint or draw the face after the dolly is sewn together.

4. Sandwich the batting between the 2 layers of kraft•tex.

By machine: Set your machine to an even zigzag stitch and stitch around the perimeter of the dolly through all 3 layers. Stitch over the outer edge to enclose the batting using a matching color thread.

Stitch zigzag over edge.

By hand: Blanket stitch around the perimeter of the dolly through all 3 layers, maintaining a distance of ⅛″–¼″ between your stitches.

Creating the Hairstyle

1. Choose a hairstyle from the patterns (pages 101 and 102) or design your own using a pattern as a guide. Photocopy or trace and cut out the associated hair shapes to form a paper template (for example, short hair front and short hair back).

2. Pin the templates to the felt pieces; then cut out the felt shapes.

3. Place hair 1 facedown and stack hair 2 (and hair 3 if applicable) faceup, aligning the rounded tops of the hair shapes.

4. Stitch around the top edges of the hair through all the layers to create a "wig." Use the pattern as a stitching guide.

By machine: Stitch using an ⅛″ seam allowance as indicated on the pattern piece.

By hand: Whipstitch or blanket-stitch around the edges.

Tip

If you want to use just one hairstyle, you can permanently affix the felt to the dolly's head using fabric glue, a hot glue gun, or fusible web.

Making the Clothing

1. Cut 2 kraft•tex pieces 5″ × 5″ for each garment.

2. Trim the fusible web to fit. Following the manufacturer's instructions, fuse the kraft•tex piece to a fabric scrap. Remember that each garment has 2 pieces, front and back, so make sure you fuse enough fabric for both.

Tip

If you want to make reversible garments, repeat the process for the exposed kraft•tex side of the sheet.

3. Photocopy or trace 2 copies of each clothing pattern (pages 101 and 102) and cut them out. Trace onto the fused kraft•tex/fabric and cut out.

4. Punch holes in the shoulders of the tops or the waist of the pants, as indicated on the pattern. *Optional:* Insert eyelets/grommets to reinforce the holes. It isn't necessary, as kraft•tex is strong and will not rip with repeated use, but it does provide a nice, finished look.

5. Cut pieces of ribbon approximately 3″ long. Cut the ends at an angle and thread them through the holes on each of the garment pieces. *Optional:* Further decorate the garments with trim and findings. Use paint, collage, embroidery stitches, or whatever embellishments you enjoy most.

6. Repeat for each garment in the dolly's wardrobe.

7. Dress the dolly by tying the ribbons together to hold the front and back garments to the dolly's body.

Have fun experimenting with different clothes and hairstyles, but remember to share the finished project with your kids!

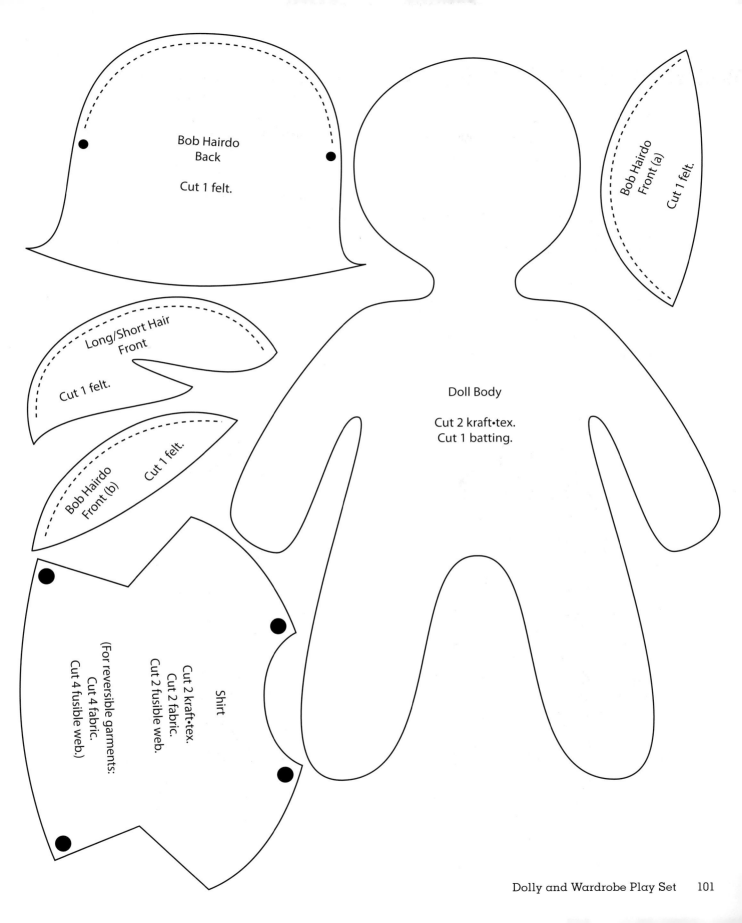

Bob Hairdo
Back

Cut 1 felt.

Bob Hairdo
Front (a)

Cut 1 felt.

Long/Short Hair
Front

Cut 1 felt.

Bob Hairdo
Front (b)

Cut 1 felt.

Doll Body

Cut 2 kraft·tex.
Cut 1 batting.

Shirt

Cut 2 kraft·tex.
Cut 2 fabric.
Cut 2 fusible web.

(For reversible garments:
Cut 4 fabric.
Cut 4 fusible web.)

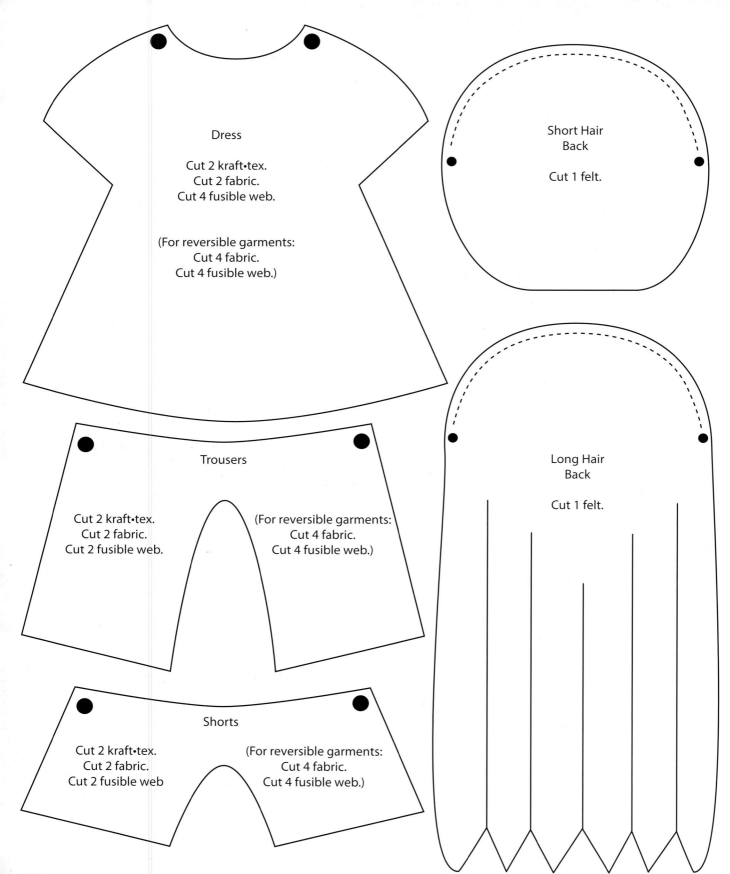

Dress

Cut 2 kraft·tex.
Cut 2 fabric.
Cut 4 fusible web.

(For reversible garments:
Cut 4 fabric.
Cut 4 fusible web.)

Short Hair
Back

Cut 1 felt.

Trousers

Cut 2 kraft·tex.
Cut 2 fabric.
Cut 2 fusible web.

(For reversible garments:
Cut 4 fabric.
Cut 4 fusible web.)

Long Hair
Back

Cut 1 felt.

Shorts

Cut 2 kraft·tex.
Cut 2 fabric.
Cut 2 fusible web

(For reversible garments:
Cut 4 fabric.
Cut 4 fusible web.)

Treasure Map

Finished map: 8″ × 10″

Artist:
Marie LeBaron

Marie LeBaron is the founder and managing editor of the popular parenting blog Make and Takes and author of the book *Make and Takes for Kids*. She's a mother of three living in Seattle. There's always some sort of project going on in her home—her kitchen table is often cluttered with crafts. When she's not crafting and creating with her kids, she loves to read, run, and blog.

Company: *Make and Takes*
Website: *makeandtakes.com*

kraft•tex is the perfect durable material for a treasure map that will last through land and sea adventures. Have fun creating your own pathway to "X marks the spot!"

MATERIALS AND SUPPLIES

- **kraft•tex:** 10″ × 12″
- **Paint, markers, colored pencils, or crayons**
- **Rub-on stickers** (*optional*)

INSTRUCTIONS

Refer to All about kraft•tex (page 4) for basic information.

1. To make the map's rustic edges, use scissors to start a tear on each corner of the kraft•tex; then tear each side with your fingers.

2. Place the kraft•tex in a sink or plastic container filled with hot water. Soak it for at least 5 minutes.

3. Take the kraft•tex out of the water and squeeze out any remaining liquid. Scrunch the entire piece for 1 or 2 minutes to give it a rough, tattered look.

4. Leave the kraft•tex scrunched while it dries completely. Flatten it out when it is dry.

5. Draw the map design with a permanent marker. Give it mountains, trees, water, and a winding path. End the path with a big X to mark the treasure's location.

6. *Optional:* Color inside the black marker lines with crayon for some extra color.

Scraps & More

Don't throw away your kraft•tex scraps! Because kraft•tex is so durable, even the smallest bits of it can be used. Betsy La Honta was challenged by the Stash Books staff to come up with projects using only kraft•tex remnants. Here are just some of her ideas.

Artist:

Betsy La Honta

See Betsy's profile in Snowflake Wallhanging (page 22).

Patches, Labels, and Tags

Refer to All about kraft•tex (page 4) for basic information.

Making patches, labels, tags, and cards is a great way to use up even the smallest pieces of kraft•tex. Pull out your craft supplies and get creative! Here are some ideas on how to use up these smallest pieces.

- Create monograms and name tags to sew onto bags, backpacks, totes, hats, and any other item you'd like to personalize. If it's a surface you can't sew on, use glue to hold the label in place.

- Whip up fun and funky patches for jackets and bags.

- Make durable labels for organizing (see Sweet Storage Boxes, page 16, for examples).

- Make fun, unique gift tags.

- Stamp a tag with your contact information to use as a luggage tag.

To make a label, patch, or tag, simply cut a scrap into the desired shape and use ink and stamps to add your design. You can use rubber stamps or metal jewelry-making stamps for added texture. Betsy used a Spellbinders Grand Calibur Machine (see Resources, page 119) to emboss some of her tags, adding a special touch. Mix and match with your favorite fabric scraps to add color.

Woven Coasters

Finished coaster: 4⅛″ × 4⅛″ or 4″ diameter (circle)

Refer to All about kraft•tex (page 4) for basic information.

1. Cut a piece of kraft•tex the desired base shape and size (square, circle, etc.). Cut strips (mine are 1″ wide) and get weaving. See Vegetable Basket Place Mats (page 10) for information on weaving.

Options include the following:

- Weave strips of the same color of kraft•tex.

- Weave strips of different colors of kraft•tex.

- Topstitch the kraft•tex strips before you weave them.

- Combine kraft•tex and felt.

- Topstitch strips of fabric or ribbon on the kraft•tex strips before you weave them.

2. Stitch the woven strips to the base and trim to size.

3. Make a strap to hold together the coasters by cutting a strip of kraft•tex to fit around the coasters with an overlap of about 1″. Sew a button on one end of the strip. Cut a buttonhole on the other end of the strip.

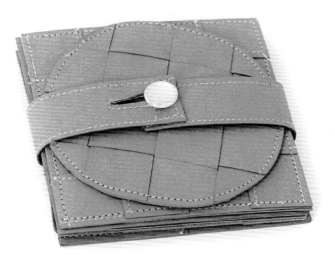

Key Fobs

Finished key fobs: varies
Finished tassel fob: 1½˝ × 4¼˝, ¾˝ × 4˝ (without hardware)

Refer to All about kraft•tex (page 4) for basic information.

To make a strap fob:

1. Decorate a strip of kraft•tex as desired: use decorative tape, fabric strips, lace, paint, or stamps; distress; or add die-cut shapes—the options are endless!

2. Fold the strip in half and trim to a straight edge. Using pliers and following the manufacturer's instructions, attach the key fob hardware.

To make a tassel fob:

1. Start with a piece of kraft•tex 3½˝ × 9˝. Score or draw a line ½˝ from the top of a long edge.

2. Create a fringe by making cuts ¼˝ apart and *up to* the ½˝ line along the entire length of the strip.

3. Fold a ¼˝ × 1½˝ kraft•tex strip in half, thread it through a round key ring, and sew it to the top ½˝ section at an end of the 9˝ strip.

4. Place a piece of double-sided tape along the top ½˝ of the 9˝ strip. Beginning with the key ring end, roll the strip firmly. When you get to the end, secure with additional glue or tape and, if desired, wrap with another strip of kraft•tex, decorative tape, or ribbon.

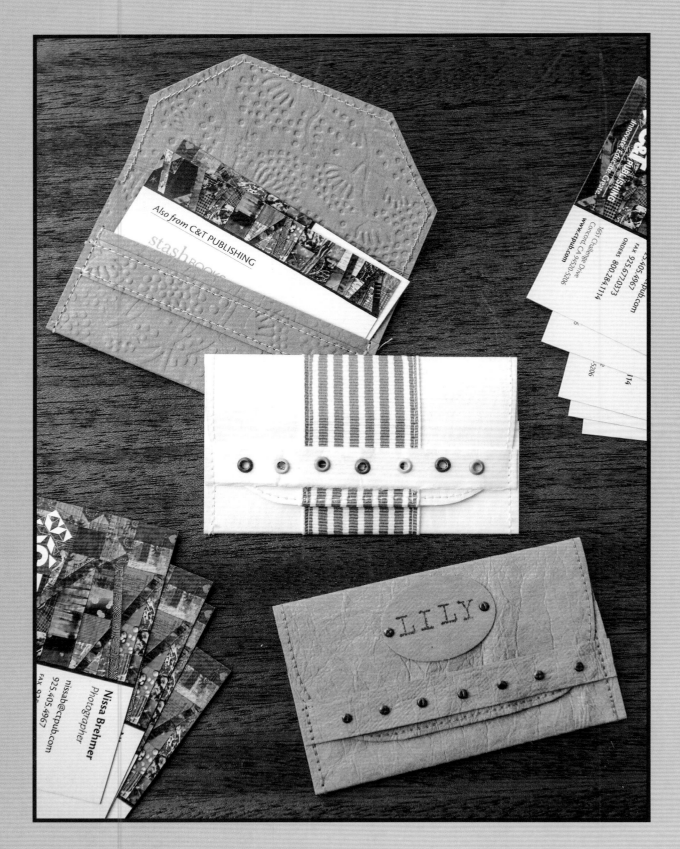

Business Card or Gift Card Holder

Finished holder: 3″ × 2½″

Refer to All about kraft•tex (page 4) for basic information.

1. Cut 1 piece of kraft•tex 4″ × 6″, and another piece ½″ × 4″ for the flap-holding strip.

Optional: Embellish, paint, or stamp, or add trims to the case and strip before sewing.

2. Fold a short end in 2″; this will be the top flap. ***Figure 1***

3. Cut the corners of the top flap at an angle or round the corners.

4. Fold the other short end in 1½″; this will be the bottom of the case. ***Figure 2***

5. With the bottom end folded up, place the ½″ × 4″ strip across it, ⅝″ from the bottom, and adjust to make sure it is in the correct position to hold down the flap. Clip the strip in place.

6. Starting at a bottom corner, with an ⅛″ seam, backstitch and sew across the strip end, then continue up and around the flap, and then back down to sew the other end of the strip in place, finishing at the corner with a backstitch. Do not stitch across the bottom of the holder. ***Figure 3***

Tuck in your cards and slip the flap under the strip.

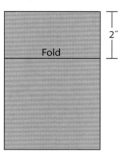

(1) Top flap fold

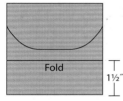

(2) Bottom fold

(3) Stitch it together.

Scissor Holster

Finished holster: varies with size of scissors

Refer to All about kraft•tex (page 4) for basic information.

Scissor holsters are an easy way to protect your scissors and keep them from poking into things they shouldn't. kraft•tex makes the holsters strong and sturdy.

1. On a kraft•tex scrap, trace all the way around your scissors, ½˝ from the edge of the scissors. Cut this shape out carefully. This will be the back piece. *Figure 1*

2. On another kraft•tex scrap, using the back piece as a guide, trace around the blade portion of the scissors. Cut out carefully. This will be the pocket. *Figure 2*

3. *Optional:* Embellish or stamp the back and pocket. You can also topstitch across the straight edge of the pocket.

4. Clip the pocket to the back, matching the edges. Topstitch ¼˝ around the edge of the entire holster. Trim ⅛˝ away from the stitching to clean finish the edges.

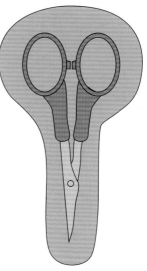

(1) Trace scissors.

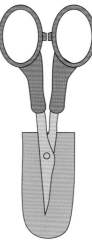

(2) Trace blades.

Pencil Case

Finished case: 3″ × 7¾″

Refer to All about kraft•tex (page 4) for basic information.

1. Cut 1 piece of kraft•tex 3″ × 10½″ for the back and 1 piece 3″ × 7¼″ for the front.

2. On the top edge of the back piece, use a drinking glass or other round object to trace a half-circle on the flap. Carefully trim, following the outline, to create rounded corners. *Figure 1*

3. On the top edge of the front piece, cut out a half-round notch using a smaller circle, if desired. *Figure 2*

4. If you are adding a patch, topstitch the decorative patch to the front of the case now; then topstitch across the top short edge of the case.

5. Cut a piece of ribbon 1″ longer than the width of the pencil case for the strap. Cut a second piece 1½″ long for the side loop.

6. Secure the front and back pieces with bulldog clips. Fold the front flap down 2½″ and mark the sides of the case with a pencil mark where the ribbon will need to go to hold the flap down.

7. Fold and finger-press an end of the ribbon approximately ½″ in. Tuck the folded end between the front and back pieces at the mark and clip together. Lay the ribbon over the flap, making sure it is straight across the case, and tuck in the other side at the opposite pencil mark between the front and back piece. Clip.

8. Fold the 1½″ piece of ribbon in half. Tuck it between the front and back pieces, approximately 3½″ from the bottom of the case, and clip, leaving about ½″ exposed.

9. Pull the flap back out and lay the pencil case flat.

10. With the case facing up, beginning at a tip corner of the front, stitch ⅛″ from the edge all the way around the case, including the top flap. Be sure to keep the ribbon ends straight and secure between the front and back pieces as you sew.

(1) Draw and cut curve.

(2) Cut half-round notch.

Bookmarks

Finished bookmarks: samples shown are 2½″ × 7¾″,
3⅛″ × 6⅞″, 3″ × 7¾″

Refer to All about kraft•tex (page 4) for basic information.

Use your imagination and any technique you like! Layer scraps of
kraft•tex with fabric, felt, and more to create fast, fun, and easy
bookmarks. Punch a hole or add a grommet to the top and finish
with a flourish of ribbon, or keep it sleek and simple. These make
great gifts—tuck one into a book or use as a gift tag.

Resources

kraft•tex and Other Materials

Bosal

Sew-in fleece
bosalonline.com

C&T Publishing

kraft•tex, Lesley Riley's TAP Transfer Artist Paper, Silicone Release Paper, Alex Anderson 4-in-1 Essential Sewing Tool
ctpub.com

The Warm Company

Steam-A-Seam 2, Warm & Natural Batting
warmcompany.com

Dyes, Paints, and Waxes

Jacquard Products

Dorland's Wax Medium, Lumiere paint, Procion MX dye
jacquardproducts.com

photoEZ Silkscreens

COLORHUE dye
Photoezsilkscreen.com

Supplies

Sizzix

Die-cut and embossing machines
sizzix.com

Spellbinders Paper Arts

Die-cut and embossing machines
spellbinderspaperarts.com

X-ACTO

Craft knives
xacto.com

Marking Tools

Clover Needlecraft

Hera Marker, Wonder Clips
clover-usa.com

Pilot Pen

FriXion Erasable Pen
Pilotpen.us